Religion and the
Ambiguities of Capitalism

RONALD H. PRESTON

Religion and the Ambiguities of Capitalism

The Pilgrim Press
Cleveland, Ohio

Originally published by SCM Press, Ltd., London. © 1991 by
Ronald H. Preston

Pilgrim Press edition published 1993
The Pilgrim Press, Cleveland, Ohio 44115

Cover design by Martha Clark

Printed in the United States of America
The paper used in this publication is acid free and meets the
minimum requirements of American National Standard for
Information Sciences-Permanence of Paper for Printed Library
Materials, ANSI Z39.48-1984

98   97   96   95   94   93   5   4   3   2   1

Library of Congress Cataloging-in-Publication Data

Preston, Ronald H., 1913–
    Religion and the ambiguities of capitalism / Ronald H.
    Preston.
       p.   cm.
    Originally published: London : SCM Press, 1991.
    Includes bibliographical references and index.
    ISBN 0-8298-0946-5 (alk. paper)
    1. Economics—Religious aspects—Christianity.
    2. Capitalism.   3. Capitalism—Religious aspects—
    Christianity.   I. Title.
    [BR115.E3P69   1993]
    261.8′5—dc20   92-43014
                                                         CIP

To
my wife, Mary, and our children
Mark, Ann and Barbara,
and our son-in-law Peter

Contents

viii

Preface

The context of this book is the collapse of the Soviet-style economies; the immediate occasion of it was an invitation in 1990 to lecture at the Vancouver School of Theology on current global economic issues in the light of this collapse, and from a Christian perspective.

One of the problems of writing in Christian ethics on current issues is that the situation changes so rapidly that the data quoted are soon out-of-date, even if the underlying issues remain relevant. For this reason I had intended in what time may remain to me to write on fundamental, and therefore perennial, issues. However, the invitation from Vancouver altered my plans. It seemed important to write in the context of this extremely fluid situation, even if the cost would be that the writing might soon appear dated. But in fact the themes discussed here may not date quickly. They are connected with long-term issues which have been one of my main preoccupations ever since I was an undergraduate. So I have tried in this book to set the immediate issues of Christian social theology in a context which goes back centuries.

I am not, of course, writing for economists. That would be presumptuous in a distant hanger-on to the discipline. Also, the data chosen to illustrate the contemporary scene are my own selection, as a committed participant in it, and carry no special authority. They are subject to all the hazards of such personal choices. My hope is that they will suggest the scale and proportions, that is to say the parameters, of the issues discussed. These are not likely to change significantly in the next few years, even if much of the data do.

The word 'religion' in the title refers to the Christian religion. It might have been better to call the book *Christianity and the Ambiguities of Capitalism*. However, in the 'West', from which this book comes, there has been the sequence of *Religion and the Rise of Capitalism* by R.H. Tawney, *Religion and the Decline of Capitalism* by

V.A. Demant, and my own *Religion and the Persistence of Capitalism* (more modest in scale). Thus it seemed wise to continue the sequence, and unlikely that this would cause misunderstanding. The theme, however, is highly relevant to all religions, for capitalism is a global phenomenon.

Since I have brought together material from different disciplines which are usually discussed apart, and in a relatively small compass at that, references could have been very extensive. I have limited the notes to works which carry the argument further on particular points, to basic sources which will lead an enquirer further, and to limited cross-references within the book. Publishers or places of publication are given if outside Britain.

The Revd Dr John Elford generously read through the whole of the manuscript with the aim of making it more readable. I am grateful to the Revd Canon Dr John Atherton and the Revd Dr P.J. ('Griff') Dines for reading Chapter 2 to test its intelligibility. It is too much to hope that there will not be defects of omission and commission for which I am responsible. My former secretary, Mrs Brenda Cole, has not lost her ability to cope with my untidy manuscripts, and I thank her for her care and interest. The editorial staff of the SCM Press have, as always, been helpful. Perhaps this is the time to express appreciation for the excellent facilities provided over the years by the John Rylands University Library of Manchester.

The far-reaching changes in the USSR which took place when this book reached the proof stage do not affect its substance, though the phrasing might have been different in some passages had they taken place in the early months of 1991.

St Anselm's Day   Ronald Haydn Preston
21 April 1991

1 An Overview

1. A plausible economic fallacy

All my adult life, one of my main concerns has been that Christian social theology should deal more effectively with the economic problems which loom large in human life and are so important for human well-being. A key aim of this book is to make a reasoned plea for a greater Christian competence in tackling these issues. This means bringing the basic themes of Christian theology alongside a competent analysis of the economic issues of our day and letting the one illuminate the other in a reciprocal relationship. Involved in this is some understanding of the fundamental economic problems which any society has to face and which are the foundations of economics as a disciplined study, and of how far economics can help to resolve them. I am certainly not expecting thoughtful Christians to be technical economists, but to have the same sort of the background knowledge as they would be likely to bring, for example, in psychology to discussions of mental disorders, or in natural science to our understanding of the universe: in other words, the background needed to cope with features on such subjects in serious newspapers and journals.

This is a modest requirement. However, economics is not in fact widely understood, and many people are frightened of it. It may well be that a book like this may prove daunting without some extra guidance. So in this chapter I propose to give an overview of the whole argument, which will be developed step by step in subsequent chapters. The amount of repetition this will involve does not seem to me to be great, and will be worthwhile if the whole book becomes clearer and easier to read.

It is a particularly opportune time to write, because the dramatic breakdown of the Soviet-style economies has caught nearly everyone by surprise. Has it left their polar opposite, the capitalist free-market economy, in sole possession of the field? But there are different versions of free-market economy. What are the problems of moving from the economy that has failed to any of the versions of the other economy? Moreover, what of the democratic socialist criticism of 'Western capitalism'? Democratic socialism has always disliked the centralized political and economic power and coercions of the Soviet system, but has tended to assume that hidden in that system is an alternative way of running an economy. That is now exploded. But what thought have the democratic socialist critics of capitalism given to the basic economic problems which are the subject matter of economics?

It is in the context of questions such as these that Christian thinking needs to be competent. Christians must aim to deal with realities and not with fantasies. Moreover, the economic realities of our world cannot be deduced from the Bible, or the history of Christian thinking on the main doctrinal themes. They can only come from empirical investigations; and that requires adequate tools. Amid the vast mass of detail in the world we should be lost without the ability to sort out different areas, and assess what are the significant details in those areas and what is trivial and of no particular significance. Economic life is one such area; and it is a test case, where much Christian thought has been inadequate and confused.

Let us take the 'preferential option for the poor', which has been widely advocated in the last twenty years. I strongly support it. I do think that the Christian gospel requires us to pay particular attention to those who are at the bottom of the social scale and experience the rough side of the economic order. Nor is it sufficient to investigate their condition from outside, as it were, like the social surveys of Charles Booth in the nineteenth century and others since. It is also necessary to give those at the bottom of the scale a platform where they can tell how economic conditions impinge on them. We have a long way to go before this is adequately done. But granted all this, it is still necessary to have a competent analysis before arriving at the best policies in the particular circumstances to alleviate, or remove, the oppressions from which the most under-privileged suffer. Those affected may or may not be in a position to arrive at these policies. It is possible that they may misunderstand the factors at work. It is possible that inadequately analysed policies designed to relieve their situation may not be the best possible, or may even make things worse. That is why I stress the importance of competence.

An autobiographical reflection provides a good illustration of the point. When I left school we were in the backwash of the great Wall Street collapse of 1929. It looked as if the capitalist system was collapsing. I wanted to understand what was happening so, not knowing anything about what was involved, I decided to read for an economics degree (with economic history) at the London School of Economics. I did not, of course, get the simple answers I naively expected; but I never regretted the choice. There I was taught by economists who were mostly Gladstonian free-trade liberals and by historians, sociologists and political theorists who were mostly some kind of socialist, and I met many students who were Marxists and challenged both, on the grounds that capitalism had indeed broken down. One could not agree with everyone and had to think for oneself. In particular I had to decide whether economics was a genuine discipline or a pseudo-one designed to justify capitalism. At the same time, through the Student Christian Movement, I became involved in the search for a social theology, and I ran into Social Credit, which was influencing many Christians at the time.

Social Credit was a theory devised by an engineer, Major C.H. Douglas, and expounded in a book, *Economic Democracy* (1920). This argued that there was a chronic deficiency in purchasing power in the capitalist system. Not enough money was earned in the various intermediate stages of production of an article to pay for the final product. Hence slumps. The solution was to give additional money grants to consumers or subsidies to producers. With these social credits the private enterprise and profit system could continue as before. This seemed delightfully simple, and on the surface plausible. There was talk of 'poverty in the midst of plenty'. We were constantly told that coffee from Brazil was being dumped in the sea because no one had the money to buy it. Social Credit appealed to many Christians as a simple way of solving the grave unemployment problem and avoiding economic conflicts between owners and workers. It was only necessary for the government to check the money power of the banks and issue credits.

This view was particularly influential in Anglican circles, chief among them the Christendom Group, which sponsored the Anglo-Catholic Summer School of Sociology and a quarterly journal

Christendom. V.A. Demant was its leading thinker and M.B. Reckitt its most popular writer. The Industrial Christian Fellowship also promulgated Social Credit in sermons and lectures throughout the country; and it dominated such publications in this area as came from the ambience of the Church of England Assembly. Most people assumed that the authors of the books and pamphlets which were produced on this economic theme knew what they were writing about. It took me a little time to find out that none of them had studied economics. It was not that they had studied economics and refuted it to their own satisfaction; they had never studied it. They assumed that economics was false and that Social Credit was correct.

When I pointed this out, I was often not believed. People could not conceive that authors could write so confidently about a subject they had never studied. It would not have happened in natural science or psychology. I had by then learned enough economics to know how the Social Credit theory could easily be refuted and why, if implemented, it would have led to gigantic inflation. I shall refer to this in Chapter 2. The Christendom Group had other weaknesses, a suspicion of international trade and a penchant for small-scale agriculture among them, but a misunderstanding of the working of capitalism was the worst, and it had serious consequences in leading many Christians fundamentally to misunderstand the grave situation in the 1930s.[1]

2. *Capitalism, social theology and economics*

I turn now from this illustration of an economic fallacy uncritically taken over by a number of Christian theologians in England to a conspectus of the development of Christian social theology in relation to the development of capitalism, as a background to understanding where we are now. This is my overview.

The Middle Ages in Europe was a relatively stable society which was both repressive and protective. In it an impressive intellectual synthesis developed in which theology was, as the phrase goes, queen of the sciences, and set the intellectual framework within which different branches of knowledge operated. A trace of this survives in some ancient universities, such as Oxford, where Doctors of Divinity take formal precedence over all other Doctors. Within mediaeval society, however, the seeds of modern capitalism in its merchant form were being sown in the Italian city states, particularly through their trade with the East. This heralded a new kind of civilization. No longer was social change to be so slow that the son could take over from his father with an assumption of continuity. Merchant capitalism was later to become industrial capitalism. Dynamic change became normal, more swift, and more pervasive, until it now embraces almost the whole world. It is a new kind of civilization in the world's history.

Classical theology had been thought out against a presumption of relative stability (St Augustine's being a partial exception). So it was not surprising that social theology was in difficulties and tended to archaism. Even in the 1662 *Book of Common Prayer* of the Church of England the General Thanksgiving refers to 'Creation, *preservation* and all the blessings of this life', before going on to give thanks for the redemption of the world through Jesus Christ. In a pre-industrial society God is not thanked for social and technological change. Nor is he, with very rare exceptions, in modern liturgies. Test-cases for social theology were the concepts of private property, slavery and usury. When the Papacy issued its first modern social encyclical in 1891, *Rerum Novarum*, it was still working with a largely unreconstructed mediaeval defence of private property, with a little help from Locke. In the debate on slavery in the nineteenth century a strong Christian defence was made of it, chiefly on biblical grounds. In the case of usury, which raises the most interesting economic issues, a long rearguard action was fought. (Because of its significance, I have treated the question in some detail in Appendix 1.)

The Reformation coincided with a great rise in prices due to the influx of bullion from the Spanish and Portuguese conquests in Latin America. There is nothing like an inflation to upset a social order, as happened in Germany in the 1920s. Those who gain are the unscrupulous and the lucky. At the time of the Reformation no one understood what was happening. Luther raged against it and harked back to a more stable mediaeval economic order. Calvin made a better attempt to come to terms with the realities of economic life. He saw that if rent on land (a static factor) was considered legitimate, there could be no ban in principle against interest on a dynamic productive loan. However, Catholic and Protestant moral theology continued as far as possible with the old teaching. In England, Anglicans and Puritans alike continued the

broad Catholic tradition of moral theology, making a few changes
(such as denying a clear distinction between venial and mortal sin),
but in social theology making as few concessions as possible to the
new economic order which was developing. The last significant
example of this teaching was *A Christian Directory, or a Summ of
Practical Theologie and Cases of Conscience* (1673) by Richard Baxter
of Kidderminster, the noted Independent minister, who was an
ecumenist before his time. He continued to treat the ethical issues
of the economic order in terms of a domestic master–servant
relationship. After that the tradition quickly faded. No precise
analysis of its failure has been made, but it seems that the forces of
the new capitalism were too strong for it, and its archaism could not
cope.

There was a vacuum in social theology just at the time that
British society began to be transformed. The vacuum can be
illustrated by John Wesley's Sermon 44 on 'The Use of Money'.
He shows no awareness of any tradition of thinking on which to
draw. He was a great admirer of Richard Baxter, but does not seem
to know of *A Christian Directory*. He appears to be approaching the
theme from scratch. He arrives at a threefold injunction: Gain all
you can. Save all you can. Give all you can. By the first he meant by
honest and legitimate means, not the amassing of wealth by
dubious ones. All the same, it is an astonishing injunction. In all the
previous centuries of Christian thought it would never have
occurred to a Christian theologian to make gaining as much money
as legitimately possible a prime aim of the disciplined Christian life.
Nor would he have produced an injunction to save. This is a quite
new Christian virtue. It is, of course, a key element in the capitalist
system, as the name implies. Setting aside resources from consumption and investing them in a process over a longer period so
that the eventual final product will be far greater in value, and thus
mobilizing savings, is an essential feature of capitalism.[2]

To give all you could, on the other hand, was part of traditional
teaching, in which almsgiving played a prominent part, though the
motives advocated for it were sometimes dubious.[3] The eighteenth
century was notable for the foundation of annual charity sermons.
Wesley himself acted on his own teaching and gave the bulk of his
wealth away. Most people took more notice of the first and perhaps
the second than of the third of his injunctions. Notice how
individualistic the teaching is. Social and economic issues are dealt

with by personal motivation and response. Strictly speaking, there is no *social* theology. Such teaching is quite different in this respect from that of previous centuries. Hence the vacuum that had developed.

England was the decisive country in the eighteenth century because it was here that capitalism was ahead. The economic theory on which it was based was mercantilism, about which it is not necessary to say more now than that it was a kind of economic nationalism. It was dissatisfaction wth mercantilism that led to the development of economics as the academic discipline that we know today. It was then called political economy, and the name especially associated with it is that of Adam Smith, whose *An Enquiry into the Nature and Causes of the Wealth of Nations* appeared in 1776. Others like Malthus and Ricardo soon followed. At the same time the utilitarian school of philosophy associated with Jeremy Bentham, James Mill and his son John Stuart Mill was developing. These were both radical reformist movements directed against what were regarded as the corrupt and effete traditional élites and institutions of the country, and were intellectually associated with one another.

The eighteenth century was an age when a well-educated gentleman amateur could make major contributions to knowledge, and this was the case with political economy. Among such amateurs were several Anglican clergy.[4] One of these, T.R. Malthus, produced a shock. His *An Essay on the Principle of Population* (1798), with its gloomy overall view of the pressure of population on susbsistence and its defence of the *status quo* as the best that divine providence could have devised, was regarded by alert Christian theologians as a scientifically established conclusion with which it was necessary for an intelligent Christian theology to come to terms. They were doing what I began this chapter by commenting on, taking for granted what they thought was an accurate diagnosis on the basis of clearly established facts. Such people are a warning to take great care that alleged facts are clearly established, and to allow for a possible range of uncertainty. In the case of Malthus there was no assured basis for his contentions that subsistence increases at an arithmetical rate and population at a geometrical rate. The first contention failed to notice the increased rate of productivity which the Industrial Revolution was already bringing about, and the second lacked biological support, failing to take into account that the rate at which humans reproduce themselves remains mysterious and often confounds demographic forecasts. Malthus's gloomy equilibrium was unfounded.

There always will be hazards in acquiring and evaluating empirical evidence. This is a human condition from which we cannot escape, and a main reason why in most cases unambiguously clear answers to questions of policy are not available to Christians or to anyone else. Decisions have to be made, as life will not wait, by judgments about many issues on the basis of the best evidence available. In the case we are considering, the efforts to provide a theodicy, or a justification of God's ways to humans, in the light of what was thought to be Malthus' scientifically established theory, led a series of writers to produce what we might call Christian political economy in the period between 1798 and 1833. The upshot was a defence of what is generally called a *laisser-faire* theory of economic life, according to which the laws of economics were as fixed and divinely ordained as the laws of physics were thought to be, so that attempts to go against them would court disaster. When the eighteenth-century hymn-writer wrote, 'Laws which never shall be broken, For their guidance he hath made', he had in mind the Newtonian universe; but the laws of economics were held to be equally unbreakable. So Christian theology gave a divine *imprimatur* to classical capitalism.

This was the situation which confronted F.D. Maurice and his group of Christian Socialists in 1848. There had been utopian social theorists in France, and Robert Owen in Scotland, all secularists; and there had been the Chartist Movement in Britain. Spurred on by these, and in reaction against Christian political economy, the Christian Socialists started a series of co-operative workshops (which soon failed). Maurice in particular taught a Christian theology one main point of which was to assert that the *laisser-faire* overall philosophy which the Christian political economists had accepted, according to which the divine plan was that humans should spend their lives competing with one another, was a lie. Most of the ideas of the Christian Socialists were inchoate, and some mistaken, but this thought was to bear fruit, and is still relevant. The immediate effect, however, was negligible, and it was only later in the century that the legacy of the Christian Socialists began to exert diverse influences.[5]

It was in the 1840s that Marx and Engels began the elaboration of a theory of 'scientific' socialism, sharply differentiating themselves from contemporary utopian, or Christian, socialisms and from the embryonic predecessors of both in the Middle Ages and the Commonwealth period in Britain. This was to have far-reaching effects in the twentieth century. It purported to show that capitalism would inevitably break down. A serious Christian engagement with Marxist thought had to wait upon the success of the Russian revolution of 1917, and had hardly begun before the economic collapse of 1929, when it did look as if capitalism was breaking down.

Towards the end of the last century economics, as we understand it, took shape. It shed the wider concerns of political economy and the utilitarian framework in which that had grown, and set out on what it thought of as a truly scientific and value-free path. This is the main theme of the next chapter. At the same time reactions against the *laisser-faire* state grew in strength. It had never been as *laisser-faire* as the theory required; for instance cholera was a factor in producing state intervention in the realm of public health. Protectionism grew, particularly in the Conservative party; and industrial workers, with increasing cohesion, refused to accept the *laisser-faire* assumptions. The fact that the economy moved in a roughly ten-year cycle of booms and slumps meant that periodically thousands of workers were thrown out of work through no fault of their own, by factors that they could not influence. Individuals had little power against management. The image of the isolated individual on a free contract was unacceptable. So the demand came for the status of a citizen with economic rights. A middle class also began to be uncomfortably aware of social ills, and it was here that the churches had their strength. The legacy of F.D. Maurice began to produce a type of thinking which led to the slow growth of the welfare state.

The process was greatly helped by a Royal Commission on the Poor Law in 1909. The previous century had spent a lot of time in devising policies to differentiate the 'deserving' from the 'undeserving' poor. The aim was to help the former and to make the conditions of the latter so uncomfortable that they would have the incentive to become 'deserving'. No one now remembers the majority report of the Commission, but the Minority Report (written by Sydney and Beatrice Webb) has become one of the classic state documents of this century. It drove a coach and horses through the distinction between deserving and undeserving, and lay

behind the reforms of the Liberal government of 1910. The two
world wars greatly accelerated the pace of social change and the
desire for reform. After the second of them the outlines of a welfare
state were achieved by the Labour government of 1945–50, but
these outlines commanded a broad consensus in the country
generally, which lasted until the Conservative government of 1979.

Since then it has been strongly challenged. It embodied two
ideas. The first was a minimum level below which no citizen would
be allowed by the state to fall. This idea is usually still supported by
critics of the welfare state, but they tend to want to reduce the level,
and make the conditions for securing it more onerous to the
claimant. The second idea was that the welfare state is not just for
the poor, but for a society in which all citizens give and take during
the various stages and ups and downs of life, sometimes giving
more and sometimes receiving more. This is a more corporate idea,
and seeks to undermine the kind of personal pride which does not
want to be 'beholden' to any one, as being a false individualism.

3. Social theology and the collapse of Soviet-style economies

Where has social theology been during these changes of thought and
institutional provision? We saw that F.D. Maurice, not dependent
on a tradition of social theology, was a pioneer in seeing the
basic falsity of the individualist philosophy, though there was no
immediate follow-up of his thought. The Pope's new start in social
theology in 1891, which I have also mentioned, did derive from a
social theological tradition, but one gravely weakened by its inability
to break free from the assumptions of a pre-capitalist society (the
teaching on usury being a good example). In fact it was because the
Pope was so mediaeval that he could see through the pretension of
nineteenth-century capitalism better than could other churches
whose tradition of social theology had collapsed two hundred years
previously. However, to deal with private property, for example, as
it had now developed, as though it were the entity envisaged by
Aquinas or even Locke in their classic defences of it, was like trying
to stop an elephant with a pea-shooter. Still, *Rerum Novarum* was
the beginning of a series of encyclicals which have gradually come
to terms with economic issues in a global context more effectively.
To them must be added other documents like the Pastoral
Constitution of the Second Vatican Council (1965), *Gaudium et*

Spes; the report of the Synod of Bishops in Rome, 'Justice in the World' (1971); and the statement of the Roman Catholic bishops of the USA on the economy (1986).[6] None of these shows a clear understanding of the working of the market as a key capitalist institution, though none of them accepts the capitalist individualist philosophy.

Not until John Paul II in his encyclicals *Laborem Exercens* (1981) and *Sollicitudo Rei Socialis* (1988) was the key assertion made of the priority of labour over capital, a point made on different grounds by Marxism. In Marxism it is based on an allegedly scientific theory of society; the Pope's assertion is based on a personalist philosophy related to a Christian stress on the dignity of the human person as a priority over an inanimate thing like capital. However, the implications of this insight are not followed through, and John Paul's encyclicals end, as do other documents, in a moral exhortation to men and women to exhibit good will in economic life, ignoring the structures in which they are placed which often prevent them doing what they would wish. Nor do these various documents face the fact that the church is so bound up with the present 'Western' economic order that it is part of the problem it is discussing, and not just the detached disinterested offerer of wisdom. Nevertheless, there is a solid basis of thought in this Roman Catholic tradition which can be fruitfully drawn upon in the future; though it would be easier if modifications to it were more readily admitted, and continuity, though important, were less stressed.

A social theology needs to draw on all the key Christian doctrines. If the first half of the nineteenth century can be called 'the age of atonement' in theology, the second half would be 'the age of the incarnation'. There is no reason why the doctrine of the atonement should not lead to a social theology, but in practice it did not. The Evangelicals who were its chief proponents were on the whole individualistic and other-worldly; where, like Shaftesbury, they did recognize particular social evils, this did not lead to a social theology. Those involved in social issues did not produce a social theology to justify what they were doing. They turned such issues into directly moral and religious ones, regarding Victorian Britain as a kind of Old Testament Israel. Slavery was to be opposed because of the opposition of slave owners to Evangelical missions, and the reform of factory hours was advocated because of the need for religious education.

The early Tractarians were also pietistic and lacked a social theology. But later, partly due to the delayed influence of Maurice, a stress on the incarnation led to the call to take the material world seriously, the world in which 'the Word was made flesh'. It was held that to think of Christianity as a 'spiritual' religion, opposed to 'materialism', was to misunderstand it. One showed one's spirituality by the right use of material things, and a wrong use of them was, in Pauline terms, 'carnal'. The call was to take seriously the corporate nature of society as constituted by persons made in the image of God, whose 'personhood' is the result of what their relation with others in community has enabled them to become.[7] Much was to come from this approach in the twentieth century, and notable names are associated with it, like the more politically liberal Charles Gore and Michael Ramsey, and the more left-wing William Temple and R.H. Tawney.[8]

In the USA the Social Gospel movement, which developed after the Civil War (or war between the states) as the country became slowly industrialized and towns grew, had rather different theological roots. It reached its best expression in the works of Walter Rauschenbusch at the end of the 1914–18 War, and collapsed in the Great Depression of 1929. A more radical social theology followed, being particularly associated from the 1930s onwards with Reinhold Niebuhr. His conviction was that it was necessary to move Left politically and Right theologically; that is to say, away from the progressive evolutionary outlook of the Social Gospel concerned with 'building the Kingdom of God on earth'.[9]

Meanwhile the incipient ecumenical movement had taken the need for a social theology seriously from the beginning. The Stockholm Conference (1925) made a start, and a major step forward was taken by the Oxford Conference on 'Church, Community and State' in 1937, which was held in the shadow of mass unemployment in the 'Western' world, Stalinism in Russia, and the Nazi and Fascist totalitarian states in Germany and Italy. Lutherans, Reformed, Orthodox and Anglicans, and the historic Peace church, contributed (with a very small Roman Catholic element) to preparatory work, producing six volumes which contain some of the most percipient social theology of this century.[10] When the World Council of Churches could be formed officially in 1948 this work continued. The first assembly was at Amsterdam that year; each successive one, at about eight-year intervals, has marked an important stage because of the preparatory consultative work done on a world-wide scale in the meantime. There have also been special conferences, like the one in Geneva in 1966 on 'Christians in the Technical and Social Revolution of our Time', which have again proved notable in the preparatory work and in the event itself.[11] The World Council of Churches has been adept at giving a hearing to groups and individuals from all over the world who normally never get one in official church channels, because it has been able to establish that these special occasions (as distinct from assemblies) are not official: they speak *to* the churches, not *for* them.

It was the Geneva conference which first alerted Christians in other parts of the world to the radically new strains coming from Latin America. At it most of those present encountered liberation theology for the first time. Liberation theology soon spread to Asia and Africa, not without some difficulties in mutual understanding, and then to Europe, North America and the remainder of the world. Most of its Latin-American proponents have in fact been trained in Europe, where they have been influenced by Marxism, the origin and intellectual foundations of which are also European. We shall be considering Marxism in Chapter 4.

Independently of the ecumenical movement, a neo-Calvinist social theology developed in Holland in the course of this century, based upon the nineteenth-century theologian Dooyewaard. Its centre is the Free University of Amsterdam (the word 'Free' in the title stands for Calvinist!), and it has spread to the Institute for Christian Studies in Toronto, and Calvin College, Grand Rapids, Michigan. It stands for what it calls 'sphere sovereignty', and wants an economics which is biblically controlled and not autonomous. In this sense it is a return to the mediaeval position based on the Bible rather than church doctrine as the parameter which controls intellectual disciplines. I think this is a mistaken project, as I hope the next chapter will show.[12].

The last few years have seen two dramatic changes. The first has been the assault on the welfare state by the New Right, especially in the UK and the USA; and by Christian supporters of the New Right on the tradition of Christian social theology which has given the welfare state general support.[13] The New Right is partly a return to nineteenth-century *laisser-faire* doctrines, but it is often combined with a nationalism and protectionism which would have been anathema to the true *laisser-faire* adherents, and makes one doubt how genuinely the doctrine is held and to what extent the movement may be an ideological cover for powerful vested interests. The apologists for it, including the Christian ones, ignore this aspect. The second dramatic change is the collapse of the Soviet-style economies. Cynics said that the aim of the Reagan era in the USA with its Star Wars project was to bankrupt the Soviet Union in its efforts to keep up, since its economy at best was only half the size of that of the USA. If so, the plan has succeeded. The reasons for the failure lie in Marxism itself, as we shall see in Chapter 4; the extent of it is greater than almost anyone foresaw. We now have the astonishing spectacle of leading Russian politicians advocating private property and a free market. The original *perestroika* economic plan drawn up by Mr Shatalin, and endorsed by Mr Gorbachev and Mr Yeltsin, begins: 'Humanity has not yet developed anything more efficient than a market economy ... the pre-requisite to ensure the effective functioning of the market includes *de jure* equality of all types of property, includng private property ... Revenue from profit should be recognized as lawful profit.'

The Soviet economy will probably take a confused route for some time, but that does not detract from such an astonishing statement. It has caught anti-capitalists off-balance. Apart from those faithful to the old-style Communist parties, socialists in other countries have never equated the Soviet centralized economic and political system with socialism. But they have tended to think that if the distorted legacy of Stalinism were taken away, a viable alternative way of running a modern economy would remain. So they have paid little or no attention to the problems of wealth-creation (as distinct from its distribution), to the role of profit, to the concept of competition, and to the role of the market as a humanly devised institution. Now they are caught out. Does this call for a market economy mean that capitalism has triumphed? Cradle socialists bemoan that the Left is abandoning 'socialism'. But what do they mean by that?

There are in fact various models of the market economy. The social market economies of Western Europe are not the same as that advocated by the ideologists of the New Right; they are a kind of managed capitalism (which the socialist ideologists of a Marxist type hold to be impossible). They have been much influenced by Christian Democratic parties who have drawn upon Roman Catholic social theology. There is also a democratic socialist model, partly worked out by theorists, partly embodied in Sweden. Interesting questions arise as to the extent of private property it allows, and about how far one can have capitalism without capitalists.

I propose to argue that the issue is not between the free market and the central, planned economy, but how far we can get the best of what the social market and democratic socialist models propose; and by democratic I mean a system whereby the government is removable by free elections, so that the policies it pursues must enable it to win power and to retain it. This is the obverse of a revolutionary proposal. Whatever may be the case in some countries, advanced and complex inter-connected industrial societies do not lend themselves to revolutions. We shall see that although the free market is an ideal model and in practice a useful human device, the ambiguities of capitalism are such that it cannot be accepted in any overall sense as a satisfactory economic order. The United Church of Christ of the USA expressed the issue cogently in 1989 when it said:

> The market is not God – and it is not Satan. It was produced in history – a socially constructed reality with great, yet specific, capabilities and very specific and great limitations. Once it is demystified, removed from the structures of heaven and hell, we can examine its capabilities and its limits and we must resist all efforts to re-mystify it.

In comparing 'Western' capitalism with Soviet-style socialism, the first Assembly of the World Council of Churches at Amsterdam in 1948 said:

> Each has made promises which it could not redeem. Communist ideology puts the emphasis on economic justice, and promises that freedom will come automatically after the completion of the revolution. Capitalism puts the emphasis upon freedom and promises that justice will follow as a by-product of free enterprise: that too is an ideology which has proved false.

The tension remains the same to-day in comparing the social market version of capitalism with the democratic version of socialism.[14]

What contribution can Christian social theology make in this situation? I shall consider certain recent contributions in Chapter 6. It must have an adequate method of moving from the Bible and from Christian doctrine to the data of the contemporary world. The history of Christian social theology is largely one of a misuse of the Bible by a refusal to put its texts in their historical context or, more accurately, to differentiate a basic witness to Jesus Christ, the same 'yesterday, to-day and for ever', as the Letter to the Hebrews says (13.8), from the bearing of this in varying historical contexts. Hence, for instance, the dismal debates on slavery or usury. Again doctrines were worked out against an assumed background of relative social stability so that the *status quo* at any time was taken as God's will. The implications of doctrine were thus interpreted conservatively, and the challenge in them to the social order was lost. Since the development of rapid social change, this has become a self-defeating process: the church is prone to defend a *status quo* which has already changed, without noticing the fact. How long will the church take in Britain to face the fact that its picture of family life, with father at work and mother occupied with home and children, is uncharacteristic?

To avoid such hazards, competence in understanding what is going on in the world is needed. I do not suggest for one moment that Christians must *approve* all that is going on. Change itself does not bring its own criteria. It can be for better or worse. But one must know as accurately as possible what is happening. And one must have a certain basic competence and certain tools at one's disposal if one is to arrive at as accurate an analysis as the often imperfect data allows. One such requirement is an understanding of the nature of economic issues.

Economics must be taken seriously, but not too seriously; and in relation to that, the market must be taken seriously, but not too seriously. It is to this theme that I turn in the next chapter where, after the overview in this chapter, I return in more detail to where we began.

2 Understanding Economics and its Limits

The range of knowledge is now so vast that even the widely read among us have only a general impression of the parts of it which we need in order to cope with a good deal of what is covered in a serious newspaper. John Stuart Mill, who died in 1883, is reported to be the last person in the British Isles who knew practically all that was to be known at the time. Since then, that has been impossible. Indeed, the growth and sub-division of intellectual disciplines and of professionalism in scholarship has become so great that many practitioners can communicate freely only within quite a narrow range of specialisms. In the vast areas that remain they are as restricted as those who perforce are not specialists in anything, sometimes more so.

Yet perhaps this picture is overdrawn. To take one example, many men and women do have a general knowledge of natural science. They can broadly follow the vast developments in radio astronomy or genetics which have characterized the last thirty years or so. Similarly, in psychology a good deal of what Jungian analytical psychology or Freudian psychoanalysis had taught has become part of the intellectual background of our time, although no doubt it has been somewhat simplified in the process. Television programmes have contributed to this, as well as journalism, and these have not diminished but rather increased the sale of books. For two years Stephen Hawking's *A Brief History of Time*, which requires the ability to cope with a good deal of mathematical physics, was near the top of non-fiction sales week by week.

However, this has not been the case with economics. The fundamental problems of human society with which economics deals are rarely understood; nor are the limitations which make it incapable *by itself* of settling any policy decisions. Of course, many more people have studied the subject at school, college or adult lectures than was the case until recently, and that increases an informed constituency. Newspapers and journals are full of comments on current economic issues, analyses of investment prospects and the state of the economy and the like. However, at a more fundamental level there is no clear awareness of basic issues. Christian social theology has also been weak in this respect. Since they lack technical competence, many theologians who write about economic issues are liable to be led astray by those who propound theories or panaceas because they do not have the equipment to evaluate them. It is important to understand some concepts basic to modern economics as it applies to ongoing discussions of public economic policy. The role economics can play is important. Understanding its limits is equally important. Economics needs to be taken seriously, but not too seriously!

1. From political economy to economics

Modern economics, as distinct from political economy, was born about a century ago. In the previous century, from the time of Adam Smith, who is usually regarded as the founder of the discipline, no great distinction was made between political and economic issues, so the name political economy was appropriate. John Stuart Mill's *Principles of Political Economy* (1848) may stand as an example. It had been predominantly concerned with large-scale problems (macro-economic ones): capital accumulation and growth, population growth, diminishing returns in agriculture, and national policies. A change came in 1871 with Stanley Jevons' *Theory of Political Economy*. It still used the same title, but the substance was different. It was concerned with narrower problems (micro-economic ones): economic choice in a situation of relative scarcity, and put in a quasi-mathematical frame. Jevons was a professor at Manchester University and responsible more than anyone else for the establishment of what became generally known as the 'Manchester school' in economics. The change of substance was marked by the change of title in Alfred Marshall's *Principles of Economics* (1890), which became a basic textbook for the next forty years. (The old term political economy is still used to refer to the discipline in some universities, but the substance is different.) It was at this time, too, that economic history became a separate academic study. The term political economy may still be needed, as we shall see, but if so, it will be used to refer to necessary elements in decision-making with which the narrower discipline of economics does not deal, involving political theory and philosophy.

Economics concentrates on the economic problems which any society has to solve: what to produce and consume among all the possibilities that theoretically exist, and how much to set aside and invest of what is currently available for the future.[1] In order to proceed at all it has to make some assumptions, without which no single study of the vast variety of human life is possible. Economics shares one assumption with all serious enquiry, that the universe is orderly and not chaotic. This is a major assumption behind which it is not possible to go; we all take it for granted, and must do so. Those who think theologically find this a profound theme for meditation, for worship and praise, and for hymns and prayers. Beyond this, economics makes two further assumptions. 1. The basic economic problem is that of choice between relatively scarce resources which have alternative uses. 2. The more of these resources we spend on particular goods and services, the less we shall desire further expenditure of resources on them rather than alternative goods and services. Something needs to be said about both assumptions.

The economist assumes that our resources are *relatively* scarce. They are, of course, absolutely scarce also, since the earth is finite. From time to time there are scares that these absolute limits have been reached, either partially or as a whole. But these scares are not well-founded.[2] There must be limits, but we have little idea of what these limits are in so far as they affect economic decisions which we have to make today. There are too many imponderable factors. But that resources are relatively scarce seems clear. There are always more things that individuals and societies want to do with their resources than they are able to. They have to choose, but on what basis shall they choose? The economic cost of what they choose is all the things they cannot do because of what they have chosen to do with their relatively scarce resources. Economists call this opportunity-costs.

The reality of the relative scarcity of economic resources is often not realized, or is denied. Marx denied it. Whilst paying tribute to the enormous increase in productivity achieved by capitalism, he held that it did not distribute enough purchasing power to consume what it produced and would collapse of its own contradictions. However, by then its productivity would have been such that the problems of relative scarcity would have been solved, and the advent of a communist society would have been made possible. So there would be no economic problems in a communist society. We shall return to Marx in Chapter 4.

Another example comes from the time of the great economic slump, after the Wall Street collapse of 1929. As I have mentioned, tales were told of coffee being dumped into the sea in Brazil because it could not be sold; American farmers were paid not to produce. 'Poverty in the midst of plenty' was the phrase. A number of Christians in Britain adopted the Social Credit theory (I referred to this in Chapter 1). The question of booms and slumps in the economic system is, of course, an important one, and needs solving for human well-being, but there is a simple fallacy in the Social Credit theory which, if implemented, would have produced gigantic inflation. It is, briefly, that enough income is earned by those working in the intermediate stages of a product from the raw material onwards, and thus adding value in each stage, to provide sufficient purchasing power in the economy to buy the final product (assuming that consumers want it, and overall stabilities in economic policies are maintained).[3]

The second assumption of economics is technically called 'diminishing marginal utility'. The assumption is that the more relatively scarce units of resources are used to secure any one economic good or service, the less they will be valued when compared with all the alternatives foregone – that is, all the other economic goods or services which could not be secured because this one had been chosen. It is the marginal unit, beyond which alternatives become more desired by consumers, which establishes what they are prepared to pay for the desired goods or service. It was the development of such marginal analysis which proved decisive in the development of economics a century ago.

Can these two assumptions be seriously challenged? If they can, economics as an intellectual discipline is overthrown, and those Christians who wrote on economics but have never bothered to study it are vindicated. In one of his mischievous moods (and he liked to shock established opinion), J.M. Keynes speculated that in a hundred years time productivity might be so great that its problems could be said to be solved (as Marx had assumed it would be when a communist society arrived), and humanity could settle down to a more virtuous way of living than the economic necessity of being so preoccupied with producing wealth.[4] More than half a century has passed, and we do not seem much nearer to that goal. Two-thirds of the world's people still need a huge effort to get them out of primary poverty. True, the dynamics of advanced industrial societies is vastly increasing productivity with a much lower input of resources, as is evident from the microchip revolution. The hope of removing such poverty from the 'two-thirds world' now becomes a possibility *if* the greater productivity is used wisely. But this is a big 'if', and one cannot be optimistic that poverty will disappear. However, even if Keynes' speculation comes true after two hundred or three hundred years, human beings are finite; time is limited for them. They would still have to choose between alternative uses for relatively scarce resources. As Denys Munby wrote in 1956:

> Economizing only arises in a world where things are scarce, and choice has to be made. In heaven no problem of scarcity arises, and in hell no possibility of choice exists; economics is a science dealing with the conditions of life in this world.[5]

As for the assumption of diminishing marginal utility, it is true that there is one case where this does not work: that of the miser. He accumulates more of the same for the sheer sake of accumulation. But the fact that this behaviour is generally regarded as eccentric and irrational is an indication that the stress on the margin does correspond to the ordinary facts of human life.

2. The market as an ideal economic model

The market is postulated as the ideal way of solving the problem of choosing between relatively scarce resources. By 'ideal', I mean a model which is abstracted from the complexities of human society to see how it would work in a 'pure' form. Markets, of course, have existed from time immemorial. What modern economics has done is to think through the implications of what is going on in a market in terms of the two basic assumptions which it has arrived at. First, it has seen the market as an ideal way of getting the myriads of human decisions in economic life made neatly by an impersonal

mechanism which ensures that what people as consumers want to
spend their relatively scarce resources on gets produced. Second,
the market reacts to changes in preferences by causing profits or
losses to be made and supply increased or reduced, as demand
increases or diminishes. The consumer is sovereign.

What is to be subject to market forces, or how far it should be
subject to them, is a matter for political decisions. Fundamental
arguments of social and political policy arise here which will be
considered later. Not long ago an American economist expressed
the question whether or not to marry in terms of benefits expected
versus opportunities foregone.[6] On the other hand, with the advent
of air conditioning, air, which until recently in human history has
been a free good, has become part of the market in wealthy
societies, which can afford to price it in terms of its temperature
and humidity.

From a strictly economic point of view the market itself is said to
be entirely value-free. It is purely a mechanism through which
consumers' preferences are registered and satisfied. What they do
in fact prefer is another matter entirely, and is not for the economist
to prescribe. Economists cannot say anything about subjective
human valuations of one economic good against another, or the
strength of one person's satisfaction against that of another. They
can only observe the weight given to these goods by what is bidden
for them in the market; this establishes their price. Yet this is a little
too simple, as we shall see shortly.

Meanwhile it should be noted that the theory of the market
cannot deal with its polar opposite, the Soviet-style command
economy, which has so spectacularly broken down because prices
in that system are arbitrarily fixed by planners and bear no relation
to consumer preferences. Yet since the basic economic problems of
the Soviet-style society are precisely the same as those of any other
society, market theorists can offer an analytical comment on the
actual working-out of the Soviet system.

The theory of the market is not, however, value free. It has two
built-in values. One, the aesthetic value of elegance, is of lesser
importance. In so far as the theory is mathematical, economics
shares in the mathematician's criterion of elegance. The more
variables that can be accommodated with the least complexities in
a diagram, the more elegant the theory is held to be. Yet mathematical sophistication may be far from the actual working of the

economy, and that is something that must be remembered when we consider the limitations of economics.

Much more important is the other value, that of economic efficiency. Implicit, where not explicit, in economics is the value of achieving the maximum volume of goods and services that can be produced by the choice of relatively scarce resources, and the avoidance of waste. However, economists are bound to admit that there are many other values, and theirs will have the priority 'other things being equal' (*caeteris paribus*).[7] Often they are not equal. It is easy to see, for instance, that a society could maximize productivity at a cost of great inhumanity in the way in which some or all of its citizens are treated. In that case efficiency in the economic sense would be pursued at a cost of 'efficiency' in a wider sense; instead of being a useful instrument for human purposes it would dominate them. What economists do wish, however, is for a society to face up to the economic cost of chosen economic inefficiencies so that the parameters of choice, especially in a democratic society, are clear and not fudged. Human beings, politicians and electorates, frequently want to have their cake and eat it. It is because economists point out the impossibility of this that their discipline has often been dubbed the 'dismal science'.

The idea of the free market is a useful intellectual device, but it is important to realize how unreal it is as a practical possibility by considering its presuppositions. First, every consumer (or perhaps a family if there is only one breadwinner) is perfectly free to make each economic decision and perfectly mobile to follow the variations in the market. Next, all consumers have perfect knowledge of the goods and services available, and are not ignorant about them to any significant extent. In other words, they are well-informed about the technical properties of goods and services, and what is the likelihood of obsolescence in a dynamic, continually changing, economy. Good communications are necessary for such requirements to be fulfilled, and while these have vastly improved recently, and are still doing so, they are a long way from what is ideally required. It must also be assumed that consumers have a rational attitude to economic choice and are not subject to impulse-buying. They must arrive at a rational balance between what is desired at the moment and what must be faced in the future. A rational calculation of risk is involved in this. It is also necessary for the purchasing power of the currency to remain stable, for without a stable unit of measurement of economic value, choice becomes a gamble.

An inherent limitation to the ideal market is that it is wholly orientated on the individual (or family) consumer. If there are wants which can only be satisfied communally, the market does not deal with them. There is no way, for instance, in which the market could provide a public open space in a city. Furthermore, it must be accepted that the income of the factors of production, land, capital and labour depend upon who owns each, and this is a complex matter involving inheritance from the past, effort expended in the present, and sheer luck. It bears no ethical relation to the contribution of particular individuals to the actual production of the goods or services. Indeed, one of the most weighty modern defenders of the free market has stressed that its economic rewards have nothing to do with the moral status of a citizen. It is solely the result of the higgling of the market, the result of a mixture of effort, ability and luck. No one can be praised or blamed for the result. No one intended it. It is the result of an impersonal process.[8]

It is evident that this purely individualist, purely logical, economic order has never been even closely approximated, nor could it be. A great deal of loose talk about the triumph of the free market and the market economy in the light of the collapse of the Soviet-style economies needs considerable qualifications. I shall be saying more about this. Meanwhile, we may note that of all the actual workings of the markets in 'Western'-style economies, the nearest to the ideal model is the financial market, particularly as it has developed in recent decades; next comes the market for commodities, and after that the capital investment market. The furthest from the ideal model is the labour market, which often takes a long time to adjust to changes in market conditions. It is no surprise that those who own only their labour are not willing to be pushed about in the same way as owners of things, such as land and capital.

3. The need to move from economics to politics

If economic efficiency is one value among many, it cannot settle any policy matter by itself, unless economic efficiency in a particular case has absolute priority over all others. That decision would itself be a political one, for it is only within some political order that the economic order can work at all, as we shall see. In practice, economic issues always lead back to political ones. That is why, when economics has given us what assistance it can, political issues must be considered. When this happens, we move to a new kind of political economy, unlike the one which preceded modern economics, involving political theory and political philosophy.

Economists have in fact often moved quickly from the value of economic efficiency to the value of freedom, but this is freedom interpreted in a very individualistic sense. The reason is that economics has developed against the background of 'Western' capitalism, with its individualistic philosophy. Protestant culture has been profoundly influenced by individualism, so that the Christian gospel has been seen through individualistic spectacles. (It has affected Roman Catholic thought, too, but not nearly to the same extent, since there it stands out sharply against a more corporate catholic tradition in social theology.) It was very revealing when Mrs Thatcher, who must have been the most self-professedly Christian British Prime Minister since Gladstone, declared in a famous interview to a women's magazine that there was no such thing as society, only individuals and their families. And her frequent references to 'the taxpayers' money', which were widely picked up in public discussion and were not explicitly challenged in Christian comment, showed how unreal the concept is: as if anything gained through work or by inheritance is somehow due to individuals in isolation, apart from the social structures which have enabled them to develop and achieve whatever they have accomplished.

As far as each person is concerned, society is held together by social structures, beginning with the family. (Person, by the way, is a much better term than individual; persons are unique, individuals are replicable.) But the family itself is part of other structures: work and political authority (local and state). These mould persons before they are able to appreciate what is happening to them. As persons develop to maturity, they become able to think themselves outside these structures and in turn attempt to mould them for the better. A narrow view of freedom takes individuality (or personhood) as given, and ignores the social institutions and traditions within which persons relate to one another and arrive at what their social relationships enable them to be. To safeguard and improve these institutions is the first priority of social policy, so that they encourage the development of more humane and just relationships between persons, and do not hinder them. Family, work and political authority are so basic to human life that they can be regarded as expressions of God's will for humanity, in that it is inconceivable that human society could exist without them.[9] We do not choose whether we will be part of them or not. We are born into them. Human beings are inherently sociable. We are not forced by fear or self-interest to join together in communities (as Hobbes in the seventeenth century thought). We are born into them.

If societies are to flourish, they need all kinds of voluntary associations, in addition to the structures of family, work and state, where citizens may relate to one another for sporting, cultural, political and other social purposes. In this sense Christian congregations, and those of other faiths, have an important part to play beyond their importance in deepening the horizons of their members in worship. Societies also need an underlying moral structure to which citizens are committed and which is fostered by their institutions. Honesty, keeping promises, a sense of justice as fairness, and a commitment to the common good have to be generally presupposed, so that the deviancy of some in betraying them is widely condemned. Indeed, how disinterested good will can be fostered in modern, pluralistic, 'Western' societies is a question raised sharply by several sociologists and social philosophers, who realize that they cannot be presumed, but have to be consciously pursued, because industrialization and urbanization have weakened the traditional social and religious bonds which did foster them.

Another fact of human life which is ignored by those who understand freedom individualistically is that every form of human association gives rise to power structures and to conflicts of interest between these power structures. Pure market theory inappropriately treats humans as it treats land, presupposing that they respond to market changes automatically.

Those who own productive capacity only in the form of their own labour power are in a position of weakness, unless they are pop stars or have some relatively scarce sporting skill. The libertarian economist Friedrich Hayek, and other defenders of market theory, deny that there is any loss of freedom in this respect, because no one is literally exercising constraint. But this individualistic understanding of freedom is too narrow. If one has scanty economic resources, one is subject to those who can exercise power in the market. Power needs checks. No one, not even the most saintly, is good enough to exercise power over others, which is why there must be checks on its exercise if abuses are to be avoided. This is in principle a strong point in Western political democratic theory.

When those who oppose the free market have drawn attention to its lack of political realism in ignoring power relationships, its advocates have replied by developing what is known as public choice theory as a counter-argument.[10] Instead of assuming that governments conceive policies in the public interest and common good, public choice theory analyses government activity in terms of the economic interests of the respective actors and groups involved in the issue. In particular, the unavowed interests of the radical intelligentsia are specially attacked, as are those of the civil service and public officials. This is hardly a new point, especially since Marx taught us to be alert to the effect of economic interest on thought and action. The ambiguities of politics are evident; it can hardly be expected to be exempt from them, since they are characteristic of every aspect of human life. Alertness to ambiguities is a necessity. In fostering the basic virtues, a wise society trains, and leaves space for, its own critics. Education and religion have an overlapping task at this point. The ambiguities of politics cannot be allowed to obscure the demands of distributive and commutative justice, which the more zealous advocates of the free market want to by-pass in the interests of leaving its impersonal processes unfettered.

Turning from political factors which economics, as distinct from political economy, ignores, we must consider defects inherent in the working of the free market if it is left to itself. Many of its defenders admit that it presupposes some moral sub-structure which it too easily takes for granted, does nothing to foster, and may thus gradually undermine. All realize that some governmental structure is required to guarantee law and order, enforce contracts, and defend against aggression. However, the most ardent defenders of the market want to keep government activity to a minimum, in part because it interferes with the freedom of the citizen (interpreted in an individualistic sense); in part because governments will not be competent to acquire the necessary knowledge (as compared with the impersonality of the market); and in part because governments are likely to add corruption to incompetence. Even on these assumptions, what are thought to be the proper parameters of government action will vary. As I have mentioned, it was cholera epidemics in the nineteenth century, which were no respecters of the rich, and spread to them from the poor, that led the government to establish public health authorities.

Left to itself, the market leads to great inequalities of income and wealth, aggravated by inheritance. The more wealth one has, the easier it is to increase it. True, the market left to itself is dynamic, and what it creates it can destroy. The saga of a family moving from rags to riches and back again in three or four generations is not unknown. Nevertheless, the inequalities at any given time are great. Since every unit of wealth in any one country at any one time has equal purchasing power in that country; those with wealth can bid for luxuries in the market (or the 'black' market), and attract relatively scarce resources to supply them, whilst the poor may scarcely be able to bid for necessities. So we have luxury flats and hovels at the same time, sometimes almost side by side. In every sphere which is privately and not publicly provided (housing, education, health and personal services), those with money can attract the resources which those without it cannot. Only deliberate policies of redistribution can alter this. This is the core of the socialist criticism of the market left to itself. Socialists want to move in an egalitarian direction (not literal equality) for the sake of fraternity, but do not want to forget freedom in doing so.[11] Advocates of the market stress freedom in its individualistic sense, though most of them do want to establish some safety net below which the poorest will not be allowed to fall.

The free market left to itself cannot cope with 'externalities': the bad effects, from a public point of view, which an entrepreneur can create without any self-cost. Pollution is an obvious example. Another example is that of those who made money in the north of England in the basic industries of the Industrial Revolution and moved away to spend their money in the south, leaving the detritus of the industry behind to blight the environment. Similarly, if the market is left to itself, life may become so expensive and unpleasant in the south-east of England that there will be a move back to parts of the north, leaving a mess behind.

How far can the market cope with our responsibilities for the future? How far are we responsible for it? It would seem that we are responsible at least as far as we can reasonably foresee, which would take us to the lifetime of our grandchildren. Here neither the market not politics serves us very well. Politicians in a democracy tend to have their sights set on the next election, and whereas pensioners have votes, children and posterity do not. Politicians do not find it easy to take longer views. The market, too, tends to be short-sighted, partly because of the sheer difficulty of forecasting in times of dynamic change. Apart from uncertainties about inflation and deflation, the market tends to discount the future to the extent that it rarely looks more than fifteen years ahead.

Questions of the ethics of risk-taking arise here. This is another example of the problems of expertise. Popular attitudes on risk are often arbitrary and irrational. Familiar risks are accepted more than unfamiliar ones, invisible ones more than visible ones. People will voluntarily accept a scale of risk (as in smoking) which they would resist being imposed on them. Perceptions of environmental risks are highly subjective, and assistance is needed in assessing relative priorities in 'green' issues. Here scientists are needed, but they differ, and can change their minds. In the end governments and public opinion have to react to one another and make the best judgments they can, in spite of inevitable uncertainties and the possibilities of new evidence. Many environmental decisions must be political ones because the market left to itself does not put any price on the aesthetic quality of a beauty spot or of a Norman village church in the way of a proposed airport. Nor does it allow for irreversible changes, such as the extinction of the dodo, or for distant risks perhaps a century ahead. Once a political decision has been made, however, it is wise to use economic tools as an element in deciding the wisdom of different possible policies in implementing it. We should not foreclose options for future generations if we can help it. This is the reason why it is a matter for concern that we have landed future generations with very long-life nuclear reactor detritus without a clearly foolproof plan for storing it.

A further defect of the market system is its tendency to move in alternative booms and slumps. In the nineteenth century this was almost in ten-year cycles. A slump presses very hard on those made redundant, especially if they are unskilled, through forces over which they have no control. Since the First World War, the booms and slumps have not been so regular, and we had the long post-1939–45 war boom until the oil-price rise of 1973. In 1929 the slump was traumatic, and 1981–83 in the United Kingdom were unhappy years. How far booms and slumps can be avoided by government policy is a matter of great controversy, but it is increasingly evident that no one government can succeed alone. Governments must co-ordinate their policies, however much old habits and the attempt to keep up the illusion of national independence may get in the way.[12]

4. *What economics can do*

There seem to be three useful and necessary contributions which economics can make towards more coherent decisions on policy. The first is to show the secondary consequences of economic policies, especially the economic cost of the alternatives foregone. One example is subsidies to agriculture. These are surprisingly popular in industrialized countries. Farmers have very effective lobbies. The rational argument for subsidies is based on security, the protection of food supplies in a time of war. (This seems to become less cogent as the international and military situation develops.) Sometimes less sensible arguments are advanced, such as the desirability of being nationally self-sufficient in food (regardless of economic cost). A romantic view of pre-industrial life may also be an unspoken factor among electorates, who do not realize how industrialized agriculture has become. Electorates are only slowly appreciating the huge cost of the common agricultural policy (CAP) of the European Community, which in order to make the small and relatively inefficient farms profitable has provided huge gains for the larger and more technically efficient ones. Technical and economic efficiency point in different directions. EC food is much dearer than it would otherwise be; and the policy has a severe effect on the exports of Third World countries. Economists have a methodological suspicion of all vested interests: those of producers versus consumers, of workers as against managers, and of all citizens who, as I have already mentioned, want to have their cake and eat it. This goes back to Adam Smith, who, in an often quoted passage in *The Wealth of Nations*, says: 'People of the same trade seldom meet together, even for merriment and diversion, but the conversation ends in a conspiracy against the public, or some contrivance to raise prices.' This is the kind of evidence which makes the doctrine of original sin (properly understood) one of the strengths of the Christian faith.

Economists can also combat popular mercantilist fallacies which have survived from the eighteenth into the twentieth century, and which provide an easy escape for governments to please their electorates by lambasting foreign countries. The assumption is that there is only a fixed amount of international trade, so that what one country gains, another loses. Hence, if one country increases exports and reduces imports, it is necessarily doing itself some good. (There is also an assumption often lurking in the background that it is somehow demeaning to export raw materials and import manufactured goods.) The GATT (General Agreement on Trade and Tariffs) trading agreements are extremely important, but they are always very difficult to negotiate because of mercantilist assumptions which seek to put shackles on international trade. The economic case for free trade is that economically it is good for a country even if that country is not followed by others. Economically, a country will gain if it sticks to trading in whatever it can do comparatively better. Productivity will differ from country to country, but trade makes them all economically better off than they would otherwise be. This theory does provide for exceptions, and there may be social and political factors or values which cause the policies of countries to override the economic case, and thus by various protective trade restrictions lower their standard of living. All the economist can do is to point to the economic cost in diminishing the amount of economic resources which could have been spent on the alternatives foregone. It is a modest but useful role.

The third useful contribution of the economist is to show what policies are incompatible with one another and what are not. The best example is the incompatibility of three things which electorates want and politicians often say they intend to provide: full employment, a stable price level (no inflation), and free collective bargaining. For example, full employment with free collective bargaining will mean a scarcity of labour which can push up labour costs without any increase in productivity. There will be more money to spend, but no more to spend it on, and therefore inflation. If this policy were persisted in, the shortage of labour in some vital areas would mean either still greater inflation or the direction of labour. In practice, policy decisions are always concerned with which mix of the three is to be aimed at, and this will vary from time to time. But the situation is made much more awkward when electorates do not realize the parameters of choice, and politicians (supposing that they understand them, which cannot be assumed) do not attempt to enlighten the electorate. The result is shadow-boxing and a lurching from one unsatisfactory expedient (because it has not been thought through completely) to another.

In 1944 the coalition government in the United Kingdom produced a White Paper on Employment Policy of which the opening sentence was: 'The Government accepts as one of their primary aims and responsibilities the maintenance of a high (*sic*) and stable level of employment after the war.' This aim was also endorsed by the social thought of the embryonic ecumenical movement. Beveridge at that time thought that 3% unemployed would be equivalent to full employment (allowing for those changing jobs); Keynes thought $4\frac{1}{2}$% would be. In fact the United Kingdom got down to $1\frac{1}{2}$% or even 1% in the long post-war boom. The result was over-full employment, too little innovation and investment, stagflation, and balance of payment crises in the 1970s.

The example of unemployment has been used to illustrate that there are always trade-offs. These ambiguities in human life are just what Christian theology would lead us to expect, with its understanding of human beings as both 'fallen' and 'free'. It is because of these ambiguities that economists are so fond of saying 'on the one hand' and 'on the other hand' when discussing policy.

5. What economics cannot do

Economics cannot by itself provide a specific and assured policy. Indeed no one can. Economics cannot do this even if economic efficiency is exalted to be the supreme value to be pursued, because of inherent uncertainties in markets (though in this case it can get nearer to an assured policy). When, as is usually the case, other values are brought in, and one or more take precedence over economic efficiency, other things are not equal, and political decisions are required.

One of the problems the economist faces is that of the complexity of human behaviour and the consequent problems in forecasting. The economy is not static, and no aspect of it can be isolated for inspection as if it were unaffected by the continuous changes in the rest. Economic theory often abstracts by assuming comparative statics. Keynes's famous *General Theory* of 1935 was conceived in terms of a closed economy without international trade. Again, monetarism has had a spell in fashion, but there is no measurement of money[13] which offers a stable and predictable relationship with spending or prices, so settling monetary targets is no substitute for the exercise of more extended judgments in formulating economic policy.[14]

Economists can extrapolate from past behaviour, but they cannot be sure that behaviour will be the same in the future. All the social sciences attempt to explain the past and the present (if they can catch up with it), but the future remains inherently uncertain. Even if two models of the current state of the economy are identical, forecasters can feed in different assumptions about, for instance, government policy or the state of world trade. Paradoxically economists have to start by *predicting* the immediate past! It will be some time before they know whether they were right about it. Published data are subject to frequent and large revisions. And they are not always adequate even then.

A theoretical problem underlying economics is how far economic-ally rational behaviour will operate. To an economist, rationality is getting the most out of your relatively scarce resources, with the least expenditure of time and money. (This is not the same thing as being logical; that is the characteristic of a computer, but because a computer lacks judgment it cannot do economics.) Great play has been made recently with a theory of rational expectations, but it means little more than that people will learn from experience. There is evidence that they do. Government policies which are expected are usually allowed for in advance, so that it is only the *unexpected* ones which will have an economic effect. This does not help the economist in forecasting. And people do not always act rationally. In the early 1970s inflation made the real rate of interest negative, yet savings in the United Kingdom and the USA showed a sharp increase.

So it remains uncertain how far rational expectations will in fact operate. That is why the accumulation of data by econometrics has not settled any controversies between economic theories. Cheap computer power has vastly increased the possibility of 'number-crunching', but the economy is too complex for it to be possible to remove the uncertainties that have been mentioned. How far, and in what circumstances, humans do deviate from economic ration-ality can be investigated with the help of sociology, psychology and anthropology; but the possibility of establishing correlations anything like secure enough to serve as a 'law' for forecasting is not very great, for there are likely to be many exceptions to any correlation proposed.

In view of these uncertainties, it is not surprising that economists advocate such a variety of policies. In 1981 a poll of British economists showd 381 in favour of and 382 against the policies then being pursued by the British government. In 1990 a poll of 1000 of them showed that 66% were against cuts in public expenditure, 64% did not think that reducing the rate of inflation should be the first target of public policy, 39% thought wages and price controls should be used to control inflation, 76% thought government expenditure was a greater stimulus to economic effort than tax cuts, and 91% thought redistribution of income was a legitimate task of government.

The conclusion is that economists by themselves have little to say about policy, but the little they do say is important. Beyond that, politics, sociology and the other social sciences are involved, and so is ethics. Behind ethics is some view of the nature and significance of human persons, and on that religions and philosophies have much to say.

3 The Response of Christian Social Theology to the Rise of Capitalism

1. Continuing the tradition

The first response was to continue the old tradition. I have mentioned that private property, slavery and usury are good examples of this. I can return to the first two later; but following upon the discussion in the previous chapter on the rise and role of modern economics, this is the point to say more about usury, because it is such a clear example of the failure of social theology to come to grips with a new situation which required a re-examination of traditional presuppositions.

Money has a role as both a medium of exchange (instead of barter) and a standard of value, enabling the price of the many different goods and services involved in economic life to be expressed in a common unit. It will be clear from the previous chapter that money, like any other economic good, is a relatively scarce resource. Once the theory of the market is understood, it seems obvious that there will be a price for using money over time (that is to say, borrowing it), and the price will represent the relative strength of the demand from those who wish to borrow as against that of the willingness of the suppliers to lend. This is expressed in the rate of interest.

It was this conclusion that traditional social theology resisted for centuries. The reason was twofold: that the Old Testament forbids taking of interest from fellow-Israelites, and that Aristotle said that money was barren; it could not breed, and therefore no charge should be made for the use of it. Aristotle, newly discovered by scholars in the Middle Ages, was thought to be the scientific classifier of nature. Hence the argument from his thought that the charging of interest was 'unnatural'. So what was thought to be 'scientific' combined with the view of those who wanted to treat the Bible as a law book to rule out usury. We tend to use the term usury today to refer to extortionate interest (which money-lenders are often held to charge for unsecured loans), but in the discussions I have been mentioning the term usury applied to any level of pure interest. The discussion was intense at the time of the Reformation, and made more intense by the inflation then, the reasons for which no one understood. (It was largely caused by the influx of bullion from Latin America.) Luther was thoroughly mediaeval in the matter of usury; Calvin was more far-seeing. As I mentioned in Chapter 1, he realized that money was becoming a characteristic form of capital in the newly developing merchant capitalist society in addition to land, which had predominated in the relatively stable mediaeval society. If there had been no objection to charging rent on land, there should not be to charging interest on money. So Calvin allowed a modest charge, with safeguards against abuse. Traditional moral theology, on the other hand, did not find it easy to be so flexible. It could not squarely face borrowing for *production*, as distinct from the need to tide over an occasional and unfortunate lack of resources for *consumption*, perhaps because of a bad harvest. Various devices were sanctioned to get round the prohibition of usury, and the discussions went on for another two hundred years or more, becoming increasingly ignored in practice, and finally expiring into desuetude. The story is so illuminating and such a warning that I am including as an appendix to this book a more detailed treatment of it.[1]

R.H. Tawney's classic study *Religion and the Rise of Capitalism* (1926)[2] is largely an account of the difficulty moral theology had in coming to terms with interest, and with the ruptures in traditional social relations which were occurring. Since, as we have noted, mediaeval society was both repressive and protective, to loosen the repression of traditional social hierarchies meant loosening the protection they offered. The end-result was a *laisser-faire* society in which protection of the status previously given to a citizen had almost gone, and individuals were left to make their own contracts in selling their labour as best they could. Out of the rebellion against this came the framework of the welfare state, which is a return to a citizen status. The issue between these two is not a fixed one; the boundaries can vary. However, it is clear that a purely contractual view of social life will not be accepted.

Tawney was thinking especially of the interminable discussion of usury when he said, 'The Church ceased to count because she ceased to think'. Teaching which should have been thought out afresh was merely repeated.[3] The result was the vacuum of social thought by the eighteenth century which was the background to Wesley's sermon on 'The Use of Money', which I mentioned in Chapter 1.

2. The vacuum: and the development of Christian political economy

The vacuum meant that in one sense, as far as Britain is concerned, religion in its predominant Protestant version had capitulated by default to capitalism.[4] The positive defence of capitalism was to come at the end of the century. But momentous economic changes were taking place in the eighteenth century, and theological challenges were made to the Christian faith which required an answer. The answers provided were on new grounds, and were not related to the now-defunct tradition of social theology.

Bernard Mandeville's *Fable of the Bees* (1714) is a good example of the new challenges which had to be faced. Its sub-title is *Public Vices – Private Benefits*. In the book, Mandeville maintains that all actions are equally vicious because they are all motivated by self-interest. This greatly influenced discussions in the eighteenth century, not only in theology, but in moral philosophy. Straddling both was Bishop Butler, who argued strongly in his *Sermons* that actions decided on the basis of benevolence and of cool self-love would prove to be the same. I shall have to say more about self-interest in considering Christian Socialist criticisms of capitalism later in this chapter, but this book is not the place to dwell on discussions in moral philosophy. Suffice it to say that Butler remains a major figure who cannot be ignored.[5]

The economic challenge was that of mercantilism, an economic doctrine congenial to unregenerate men and women then and today. It was not primarily concerned with the acquisition of bullion, which was Adam Smith's charge against it, but with the idea of a favourable balance of trade, and the belief that one nation can gain economically only at the expense of others. The assumption was that there is a fixed amount of international trade. One can still find a similar assumption in the media almost any day in reports on remarks of politicians about trade talks, such as those of GATT (the General Agreement on Trade and Tariffs), and in the opinions of many businessmen. The attack on mercantilism in the eighteenth century, as political economy developed, was accompanied by one on corruption, government inefficiency and the privileges of an effete élite; today the economic case against it is important.

Clergy were among those who contributed to the development of political economy. Intelligent amateurs could do this before the subject became a professional discipline.[6] Josiah Tucker (1712–99) is an example. He ruled out mercantilism on theological grounds, those of Christian universalism. God could not have ordered the world so that states could prosper only at the expense of one another. Nevertheless, laws were needed to ensure that the pursuit of self-interest also promoted the public good. This sentiment calls to mind the remark of William Temple in his famous wartime Penguin book *Christianity and Social Order* (1976 edition, p. 65) that 'the art of government in fact is the art of so ordering life that self interest prompts what justice demands'.[7]

Adam Smith, whose *An Enquiry into the Nature and Causes of the Wealth of Nations* (1776) is probably the most influential book on economics ever written, was also no uncritical supporter of crude self-interest. He recognized its power as a driving force in human affairs and considered how it could be harnessed so that private gain resulted in public good. His solution was a competitive market underpinned by morality, customs and education, and a belief in a 'hidden hand' which would see that the potentially destructive aspects of competitive aggression resulted in the public good; this was a resort to the kind of God postulated by eighteenth-century Deism. Governments should provide defence, domestic protection against force and fraud, and 'certain public works and certain public institutions which it can never be for the interest of any individual, or small number of individuals, to erect and maintain'. This recognizes the 'free rider' problem, where people want to consume a good or service which must be provided for everybody or not at all, but to let others pay for it.

Smith's position could include a wide range of other public provisions. It would recognize what the economist calls 'externalities', such as the effects on the general public of private enterprises in the case of pollution. And it goes further. Adam Smith was thinking of roads, education and poor relief. But the fact that the economy has changed so much in the scale of enterprises, with giant international companies, and with the organization of management, labour and the professions into representative bodies, means that Smith's provisos have more far-reaching implications now than in his day. This is what advocates of a Smithian 'free-enterprise' economy, such as the Adam Smith Institute, ignore.

The biggest clerical impetus to the development of political economy and a Christian appraisal of it was Malthus's *Essay on Population* (1798). Its occasion was Godwin's *Enquiry Concerning Political Justice*, which was based on an utopian belief in human perfectibility. Against this Malthus argued for the inevitability of the *status quo*. He was drawing on a Christian understanding of sin which suggested that its most subtle effects are not flamboyant ones but the corruption of virtues. This would rule out the hope not of human progress but of human perfectibility. Malthus, however, went further and produced a 'scientific' theory that the food supply increases only in an arithmetic progression, whilst population increased by a geometric one, so that poverty is inevitable; any attempt to interfere with the 'natural' disciplines which rule in society would fail, and society would revert to the *status quo*. In the first edition an 'invisible hand' was brought in to show that this *status quo* was in fact an optimum, but Malthus withdrew these chapters in the second edition.

Others took up the task of producing a theodicy of the *status quo*: that is to say, justifying the ways of God to humankind in the face of what was thought to be a 'scientific' analysis of the economic order with which theology must come to terms, on the assumption that the laws of the new economics were as fixed as those of physics and must be ordained by God. Richard Whateley is an example. He accepted the Drummond Chair of Political Economy at Oxford[8] on the grounds that economics was getting into the hands of non-Christians so that among Christians there was a bias against the creation of wealth, and that it was important that political economy should not be seen as unfavourable to religion. Indeed a major objection to the introduction of economics at Oxford was that it narrowed the understanding of humanity. Whateley argued that chaos did not result from the pursuit by each of his own interests, and that free trade produced harmony, so that God must have planned the outcome in ordaining economic laws (the 'hidden' or 'invisible' hand again).

3. The Christian Socialist critique of capitalism

Christian political economy was the dominant strain in socal theology in the 1840s, with its legitimation of *laisser-faire* doctrines. It was this that the Christian Socialists challenged. They were a small but remarkable group, each of whom in the decades from 1850 made a major contribution in different ways to British intellectual life, and to the development of such institutions as Friendly Societies and Co-operatives. Their initial contribution in what is generally called the Christian Socialist Movement of 1848–54 was vigorous, but intellectually confused and, in the shape of co-operative workshops, practically unsuccessful. However, one major affirmation of F.D. Maurice remained as a legacy for the future, that competition erected as an overall philosophy of human relations in society was not a law of God but a lie. After a period of considerable economic growth and public confidence in the middle of the century, when this affirmation was dormant, it was picked up again in the last decades. By then industrialism had developed further, and its unsteady movement in roughly ten-year cycles of booms and slumps was producing social distresses which could not be ignored. Some Christian critics called themselves socialist explicitly; more were liberal-radical crusaders against selected abuses, but all could trace some influence going back to F.D. Maurice. Other influences were Oxford idealist philosophers like B. Bosanquet and T.H. Green, and the gathering of factual information by social surveys, like that of Charles Booth on London life and labour.[9] Whether the Christian critiques of capitalism were socialist or just social, over the decades at the end of the last century and increasingly in this century, the criticisms have tended to be on four grounds, which we need to consider.

1. Competition as such is suspect. It has a bad effect on human character, encouraging acquisitiveness, covetousness and insensitivity. Its opposite, co-operation, should be the basis of economic life. Sometimes the kingdom of God in the Gospels was interpreted as a 'co-operative commonwealth' which Jesus urged and empowered us to build. Not much of this is heard now, because New Testament studies have made it clear that the kingdom of God, a

central feature of Jesus' teaching, is not the outline of a social order which we are to be building bit by bit down the centuries, but a vivid picture of God's way of continually exercising his rule in the world as king. It is expressed in both the teaching and the actions of Jesus; and it is paradoxical by conventional human ways of reckoning. That is why it ended in the putting to death of Jesus.

Those who talked of the co-operative commonwealth did not spell out its parameters. Actual expressions of co-operation have broadly taken the form of producers' co-operatives, in which the workers are the owners of the enterprise, or consumers' co-operation, in which the consumers of the product own the enterprise and employ the workers in shops and factories. The second is by far the most important in 'Western' countries. When the talk is of 'the Co-op', that is what is usually meant. Producers' co-operatives have often worked with farmers, though they are often more a collection of almost family concerns than workers in a factory owning the enterprise. There are few large-scale examples of producers' co-operatives, the chief example being the Mondragon co-operative in north-west Spain, which has about 18,000 members.[10] Both are possible ways of organizing an enterprise within a predominantly market economy, and within either a public or a private sector in such an economy. Neither is likely to be the sole way of organizing such an enterprise; and in any case, elements of competition are still present in the total economic milieu.

But what is wrong with competition? Some people carry opposition to it to the extreme of opposing competitive games because in them some must be losers. This is an unreal attitude. There must be a division of labour in human society once we get beyond a scarcely imaginable primitive society of food gatherers. Not everyone can or should do everything. Selection of activities means that in a rough and ready way those who have particular talents will tend towards the activities which require the talents. This happens at the level of the family, whether extended or nuclear, and more markedly as the economic area becomes bigger and more variegated. Selection involves grading, and grading involves competition. This is a fundamental feature in human life. Humans have to learn how to be losers (and winners): that is to say, how to handle failure and how to handle success; how to regard successes and failures as relative; and how those more talented and those less talented are to live together in a community which holds together in the kind of fraternity which encourages each to make his or her own personal contribution, and does not neglect the less gifted.

Nevertheless, competition has to be handled with care because it does easily foster unpleasant qualities. I shall return to this. Its chief flaw is when it is erected into an overall individualistic philosophy. It has been a defect of Protestantism as it has developed under the influence of capitalism, rather than in the thought of Luther or Calvin, that it has seen the force of the stress on individual responsibility, but has been blind to the social setting in which the responsibility has to be exercised. For it is true that we must in the end take personal responsibility for our decisions, unless we are seriously ill mentally, or seriously mentally handicapped. No one can live our lives for us.

In the Christian doctrine of conscience it is clear that we must follow our conscientious judgments on questions of good and bad, right and wrong; and we must be responsible for having a sensitive conscience, so that our judgments are wise and discerning and not partial and prejudiced. But all this arises out of living in a social context. Society is much more than a statistical aggregate of individuals engaged in voluntary economic and cultural exchanges. Society is greater than the sum of the individuals who compose it. Society is prior to the individual. We have already noted that we are born into structures of sex and family life, of work, of political authority (and of culture), which mould us profoundly before we are old enough to realize the fact. In maturity we are able at least partially to transcend these structures, to evaluate them (for they are all ambiguous), and to ask ourselves how far they need reform, and how we should use what influence we possess to reform them. What we are able to become by the exercise of our personal responsbility is greatly affected by the influences of the structures of social relationships in which we have been involved from infancy onwards. The more humane and just they have been, the deeper will be the quality of the mutuality of our adult life. All these structures operate at the same time both as structures of grace and structures of sin; human life is a never-ending quest to strengthen the aspect of grace and lessen the aspect of sin. In terms of the state, well-motivated and co-operative citizens are a social priority. Structures are needed which help people to like one another, and which encourage those who are not socially minded to co-operate.

2. It is held that profits are suspect. The slogan has been 'production for use and not for profit'. But what is wrong with a surplus or a fee? The making of profits in a market system is an indication of what consumers want to spend their relatively scarce resources on. Losses are made by producing what, or too much of what, they do not want to spend them on. The alternative is to decide what to produce by a centralized command system, or by rationing. The command system is extremely complicated and inflexible, and is breaking down where it has been tried. If the planners decide to produce too much of any economic good or service, they have the cumbersome job of adjusting all down the line to a glut; if they decide to produce too little, there will be queues, and distribution will go to those who queue early or devote more time to queueing. Rationing as a method of distribution has its place in certain circumstances for standard and basic goods and services, but it easily leads to a black market. Rationing as a general method of distribution, except in extreme circumstances, is highly cumbersome, inflexible, and prone to corruptions of power. Profit as a *directive* as to what is to be produced by our relatively scarce resources, as in the market system, remains the least bad way of organizing the economic order. What is done with the profit is, of course, important. It is possible to imagine an economic order which is run by profit-criteria but where the profits are spent communally and not privately, but that is far-fetched, and as a model subject to the disadvantages of cumbersomeness, inflexibility and corruption already mentioned. So profits are likely to be used as a private *incentive* as well as a directive. This brings us back to the questions of motivation and human character, and to the question I have just raised. What is wrong with making a surplus (a profit) as a result of producing something that others indicate they want, by the extent of their willingness to spend their relatively scarce resources on it? This leads to the third criticism of capitalism.

3. The motive for engaging in economic activity should be 'service, not self'. A suspicion of the self is hidden in this slogan. The concept of the self needs elucidation. To begin with, there is the point made by developmental psychology that in order to relate fully to others we need to have a self which can be called mature, or integrated. It is not a new point. Jesus summed up the Old Testament Torah in two commandments, the second of which is 'You must love your neighbour as yourself'. Granted that, the

prime issue is one of a proper mutuality in the relation of oneself to others. The aim of the Christian life is not self-sacrifice for its own sake, but a service to the neighbour, which may indeed involve sacrifice but may also lead to mutual fulfilment. More than that, the notion of self-interest needs to be considered carefully. It does not necessarily mean selfishness, but a thought-out pursuit of one's projects. These can vary between degrees of egoism and altruism, but, as Bishop Butler maintained, a well thought-out pursuit of either is likely to lead to much the same action. Appeals to self-interest are often short-sighted. Appeals to altruism are necessary to strengthen the ability humans already have to consider the interet of others, and to take a less narrow view of their own. Capitalist society does not pay enough attention to this, or it would take steps to provide a more adequate minimal standard of living for everyone.[11]

But a complex economic order cannot be based on the pre-supposition that everyone, no matter what their religious faith or philosophy, will act on the far-sighted self-interest which in practice approximates to benevolence. 'Service, not self' is too simple a slogan. It is legitimate to make a provisional assumption that providing a good or service (by honest means) which a 'neighbour' shows he or she desires by being willing to spend enough of his or her relatively scarce resources to pay for it is a way of expressing love both of the self and of the neighbour. The market is the least bad way of finding out over a wide range of economic goods and services what love of neighbour in economic terms requires. There is the famous illustration of Luther, in discussing Christian vocation, that a cobbler who cobbles his neighbour's shoes efficiently is being a Christ to him, and there can be no higher vocation than that. But of course the market can have inadequacies and distortions. They will be considered later.

4. Capitalism mistakenly treats labour as a thing, like land and capital. In the case of labour, human factors make a simple reliance on changes of supply and demand inappropriate. Humans do not exist to serve the economic system; the system exists to serve humans. This is where the strong moral note in Marxism speaks forcefully, with its talk of alienation of the human being and the inhumanity of the cash nexus. Humans have personal preferences, and the maximizing of earnings is not always the chief one. Humans have motives, and their productivity depends partly on

their motivation and not just on their technical equipment. Humans are consumers as well as producers, so that they have the complexity of two vested interests: in the conditions and pay in their jobs as producers, and in economic efficiency as consumers of all the rest of the goods and services they use. In the case of humans their human capital cannot be separated from their person. They are not as mobile as capital, and should not be.[12]

The upshot of these four criticisms is that though much criticism is ill-founded, there is enough reason to raise serious questions about capitalism. It is an ambiguous phenomenon. In the early days of the ecumenical movement the famous Oxford Conference on 'Church, Community and State' in 1937 said of capitalism in its section on economic life that it encouraged acquisitiveness and the use of irresponsible economic power, and frustrated a sense of vocation; its individualism and inequalities led to a lack of fraternity.[13] There is a germ here of much that has been refined since then.

But what is the alternative? Here the explicitly Christian Socialist movement has not been very helpful. Its latest manifesto, dated 1980,[14] refers to five points:

1. Equality of opportunity. This is a liberal-radical aim, but not a socialist one. Effete privilege is indeed a scandal, but a society merely based on careers open to the talented would be a meritocracy and most unpleasant. The less gifted majority would be relatively neglected and there would be little fraternity.[15]

2. Workers' ownership. This stresses only the interest of workers as producers, and forgets their interests as consumers. Workers' ownership easily falls prey to a lack of dynamism in the interest of preserving existing jobs. Instead of expansion when it is needed, the workers tend to want to keep others out, and increase their own returns rather than employ newcomers; in times of recession they tend to resist change and try to hang on to things as they are. Workers' ownership has its place, but as one element only in the economic order.

3. Community control of wealth. It is not clear what this means. Are there to be private incomes but no private wealth? Does this mean the end of inheritance? Or does 'community control' merely mean that the government has power to regulate inheritance by death duties and the like? This is a minimum interpretation, and only the most extreme *laisser-faire* advocate would reject it. Inequalities of wealth are much tougher to deal with than

those of income, and they constitute a problem to which we will return.

4. A planned socialist economy. This is what has collapsed in Soviet Russia and Eastern Europe. It is akin to the famous Clause 4 of the Labour Party, which refers to the public owner-ship of all the means of production, distribution and exchanges, and which remains as a historical reminder of the Labour Party's roots, as does the singing of the 'Red Flag' at the annual Party Conference. Like the Thirty-Nine Articles of the Church of England, it has to be re-thought in a new context today.

5. Full participation in decision-making. Men and women should indeed have a part to play in decisions which affect their well-being, but not a veto; the interests of others have to be considered, too. And that part can seldom be by direct decision-making (like calling for or ending a strike by mass meetings outside factory gates). It has to be representative democracy. A long search goes on for the best method of political representation, for all have disadvantages as well as advantages, as witness the various suggested schemes of proportional re-presentation. In industry, offices and services, much thought and experimentation is still required. This was shown when the World Council of Churches was carrying out a study programme on the 'Just, Participatory and Sustainable Society' before the Vancouver Assembly of 1983. It had made little progress on the participatory side before it abandoned it after the Assembly to concentrate on 'Justice, Peace and the Integrity of Creation'.

The conclusion of this discussion appears to be that the pure theory of *laisser-faire* is indeed an un-Christian view of human relations, because it treats persons as things. Nevertheless, the market is a creative human invention, superior to any alternative economic system in terms of life-expectancy and positive economic freedoms for humans. But it needs to be set in a firm framework of controls, involving redistribution of income and wealth by public policy in order to achieve a mutuality between citizens in dealing with the basics of life, and the crippling uncertainties with which any one of us may be faced from time to time. This may well not lead to the maximization of the productivity of relatively scarce economic resources. But efficiency in the economic sense is not the sole or the most important criterion, even though it is one which we neglect at our peril. Marxist socialism is not an option, as we shall see in the next chapter. What possible options there are will be considered in Chapter 5.

4 The Marxist Response to the Rise of Capitalism

It is hard to exaggerate the significance of Marxism as a historical phenomenon. The speed of the spread of its influence in ideas and political power since the publication of the *Communist Manifesto* in 1848 is unparalleled. The literature on it is vast. It has cast a spell on many of the best minds in the 'Western' world, out of which it came and which its aim has been to undermine. Christians could not ignore it, though their reactions have too often consisted in a simplistic dismissal of it as atheist and materialistic, forgetting Simone Weil's wise remark that there are two kinds of atheism, one of which is a purification of the concept of God. Serious dialogue between Christianity and Marxism has been rare. When it has taken place, the economic elements in Marxist theories have played little part. It is these which are my main concern in this book. The dramatic collapse of the Soviet-style economies has brought out how flawed they are. Moreover, the flaws in one section of the theories, which claim to be a unified whole, cast doubt on the entire structure of Marxism; and it is not too much to say that it is an overall ideology which has collapsed, leaving a vacuum crying out to be filled. Talk of 'the God that failed', the title of a book concerned with some ex-Marxists a generation ago, now applies to whole societies. Our discussion can be relatively brief, even though it is necessary to put Marxist economic theories in the wider context of Marxism as a whole.

1. The 'scientific' economic and political theories of Marxism

The essential point to remember is that Marxism claims to be 'scientific' socialism, contrary to all previous types of socialist thought, whether of communitarian chiliastic sects (which have cropped up at times in Christian history), or of the French utopians, like Saint-Simon, Blanc and Fourier of the early nineteenth century. Engels' well-known words at Marx's funeral express this claim well: 'Just as Darwin discovered the laws of development of organic nature, so Marx discovered the laws of development of human history.' A classic statement of the claim is also found in Engels' *Socialism, Utopian and Scientific* (1880). Marx, himself, in the Preface to *Das Kapital* (1867), refers to the 'natural laws of capitalist production working with iron necessity towards inevitable results'. He compared his method with that of physics, as did the defenders of *laisser-faire*, including its Christian apologists, though Marx turned the tables on them by promulgating different 'laws' of society from theirs.

By 'scientific' is meant laws of historical change in society which are sufficiently certain to be used as the basis of prediction. I shall return to this in more detail, but we can note how odd it is that there should have been so much disagreement over the meaning of theories making this claim. In a book *Towards an Understanding of Karl Marx* (1933), Sidney Hook included a section, 'The Quest of the Historical Marx', modelled on Albert Schweitzer's famous book at the turn of the century, *The Quest of the Historical Jesus*. This pointed out there were four Marxist groups, all claiming to be the authentic heirs of Marx: the Anarchists; the Social Democrats of continental Europe, especially Germany; the Trotskyites; and the Lenin-Stalinists, who had won in the USSR and were by far the most powerful. Since then there has been a running discussion between advocates of a more 'humanist' and those of a more 'scientific' Marx. It was furthered by the publication of Marx's Paris manuscripts of 1844 in 1932, and his *Grundrisse* in 1972 (which was a try-out for what was later to be in *Das Kapital*).

The Paris manuscripts showed a more humanist Marx (some say that Marx became a Marxist in 1845). It was to them that the more liberal Marxists of the recent past, notably the Frankfurt School associated with M. Horkheimer, T.W. Adorno and J. Habermas, appealed as the key to interpreting his work. On the other hand, *The Communist Manifesto* seemed to mark a change to a more 'scientific' Marx, though it is doubtful whether the shift was very great. The chief recent advocate of this Marx was Lous Althusser in his *For Marx* (1965) and other works, which greatly influenced the tumultuous protests in France in 1968. Althusser wanted to overthrow what he regarded as woolly and sentimental, humanist Leftists, as well as unscientific Stalinist dogmatists.

In considering Marx's economic theories, we are not bound to take sides in this controversy, though it is undoubtedly its 'scientific' appeal which has been strong; when we come to analyse that, we may find that it throws light on the revisionists who stress the humanist Marx. The fact is that Marxism has had such a varied history that its basic concepts have been subject to many rival interpretations, often arrived at after bitter quarrels over 'revisionism'.

In Marxism there are three economic and three political theories. I take the economic theories first.

1. *The labour theory of value.* According to this, the value of an economic good is the amount of 'socially necessary labour time' involved in its production.

2. *The theory of capitalist development.* This value is not paid to the worker, who gets less; and the 'surplus value', over and above what is paid, is filched by the capitalist. For this reason there is not enough money in the capitalist system to buy what it produces (an underconsumption theory which was to be picked up by others, including advocates of Social Credit). So there is a drive for markets overseas to dispose of what cannot be sold at home.[1]

3. *The theory of capitalist crises.* The rich will get richer and the poor poorer as capitalism lurches on, until the rich are overthrown and, in the phrase of *Das Kapital*, 'the expropriators are expropriated'.

Marx had no theory of how to run a communist society. He held that capitalism would have fulfilled its historic role in vastly increasing productivity and overcoming scarcity. He had a certain admiration for it. Its success would make communism possble. The state (like religion) would wither away. 'In communist society ... society regulates the general production and thus makes it possible for us to do one thing today and another tomorrow, to hunt in the morning, fish in the afternoon, rear cattle in the evening, criticize after dinner, just as I have a mind ...'[2] Only then could the slogan 'From each according to his ability, to each according to his need' be fulfilled. This absence of an economic theory in a communist society spills over into uncertainty in Marxism on how to run an economy on the way to communism. Theoretically, the USSR has been a dictatorship of the proletariat, established after the successful revolution of 1917, working towards a communist society when all internal and external class enemies have been overcome. Theoretical discussions on economic policy have been hamstrung by having to take place within the framework of these Marxist economic theories (as they still are in China), and in practice the confusions which have resulted have shown the applicability of the 'bourgeois' economic theories of the market which we have discussed.[3] (Marx was dismissive of economists, calling them 'hired prizefighters'!)

I turn now to the three political theories of Marxism, which are closely related to the economic ones.

1. *The class origins of the state.* Primitive society was communist. Then private property entered. Out of this came classes. Out of classes came the state. In communist society there will be no classes and therefore no state. So there is also no theory of politics in the communist society. 'People will gradually become accustomed to observe the elementary rules of social intercourse that have been known for centuries and repeated for thousands of years in all copy-book maxims – without force, without coercion, without subordination.'[4]

2. *The materialist conception of history.* It is the 'relations of production' which are decisive in moving history on. 'It is not the conciousness of man that determines his being but on the contrary his social being that determines his consciousness.'[5]

3. *The theory of class struggle.* After the lapse from primitive communism through the occurrences of private property, classes developed, and it is their struggles which move history on (or rather *pre*-history, for we are near the closing stage of the pre-history of humanity). This struggle proceeds dialectically: that is to say, a given state of it, the thesis, produces its opposite, the antithesis; and out of the struggle between them a new situation, the synthesis, arises, containing elements of both, but transcending either. The new synthesis again produces its antithesis, and so the struggle goes on, not in an even progression but by a dialectical progression until the end of pre-history. Marx's illustration of this is virtually the rise of the bourgeousie against feudalism, and its projected fall in the workers' revolution.

2. The sources of Marxism

It will be clear that Marxism, including Marxist economics, is not scientific in the sense claimed. Let us consider its sources. The first is undoubtedly Malthus. We have already considered the effect of his theory, and the scientific status it was given by many for several decades. His view greatly influenced David Ricardo's *On the Principles of Political Economy and Taxation* (1817). Nearly all of Marx's economics can be found here. Because population increases geometrically and food production only arithmetically, there is a recourse to ever poorer soils, and more and more of the proceeds of industry will go to the landlord in economic rent. The division between the labourer and the capitalist is determined by the 'iron law' of wages, which keeps the labourer at subsistence level. All the expenses of production could be resolved into the toil and sacrifices of labour. A contemporary economist, Nassau Senior, also wrote of the 'wages fund', according to which wages are determined by the relation between the number of the labouring population and the volume of circulating capital available for its support.

Then there was Engels. In 1844, at the age of twenty-three, he wrote an *Outline of a Critique of Political Economy*, when he was in Manchester for his first visit to his father's factory. This precedes all Marx's economic writings and has three of the least invalid of his economic theories: the periodical crises in economic development (a ten-year cycle of boom and slump); the implications of technological change; and the great concentration of industrial units. For all of these he claimed scientific certainty. He did not have the labour theory of value or the theory of surplus value.

In his *The Condition of the Working Class in England* (1844) Engels was also a pioneer in the investigation of the social effects of industrial capitalism, with data largely based on Manchester. It was the precursor of other private investigations, like that of Charles Booth and public Blue Books later in the century.

The influence of Hegel's philosophy is also central. According to Hegel's purposive view of history, Spirit was progressively revealing itself in human life and institutions. Marx turned this on its head and injected purpose into the material relations of production behind the class struggle. That is the philosophy with which his economic and political theories are surrounded. It is usually called dialectical materialism, although that is not a term used by Marx himself; he referred to historical materialism. Behind both lies an idea of progress in human affairs deriving in the immediate past from the Enlightenment, itself a secularization of some strains in Christian theology. According to this, human actors are agents of a process in history of which they are unconscious. Another example of the idea is the Whig interpretation of English history as leading willy-nilly to the current forms of political democracy, of which the historians in question approved.

Lastly, the influence of Darwin and the prestige of natural science must be noted. Today we have come to realize that there is an element of uncertainty and randomness at some micro-levels of nature as understood by physics. In the last century the ideal of physical laws was more fixed. They were all thought to be like, for instance, the law that water boils at a certain temperature at a given altitude. One can rely on this as a sure scientific prediction. Hence the point of the claim to have established laws of the same certainty in social, political and economic affairs.

What this claim failed to predict is notorious, and we need not dwell on it. Chief examples include the enormous rise in the absolute standard of living of vastly greater populations in capitalist countries, rather than the rich getting richer and poor poorer. (Relative standards of living, and the extent of the divide between rich and poor are another question.) Then there has been the rise of a huge middle class of managers and professional people between labourers and capitalists. There is also the fact that the revolution occurred in Russia, industrially the most backward capitalist country and not the most advanced, so that its problem was to drag along a reluctant peasantry rather than rely on a victorious urban proletariat. In fact communist parties have continually been caught out by events, one of the most notable examples being the Nazi–Soviet pact of 1939. Afterwards, unexpected events can be rationalized into theory, and that is how Marxists have adjusted to these major unexpected developments; but that is not much use if one is supposed to have a scientific theory with predictive power.

There has, however, been enough plausibility in Marxist theories for them to mislead. That is why they have had such a powerful world-wide influence. Now they are seen as oppressive in Eastern Europe, though still as liberating in Africa. One example of plausibility is the Marxist theory of underconsumption to account for the periodic capitalist slumps. The concept of class is a better one. In the nineteenth century, class interests were regarded as an irrational obstacle to reform. The remedy was greater rationality. In practice, this was thought to mean an intellectual élite whose judgment would carry weight with the electorate as that of a skilled physician does with his patients. Better education is the way to 'pure' judgments. This attitude was deeply rooted among the better educated. We have seen that it was central to the thought of F.D. Maurice: workers needed to be educated to be fit to exercise responsibility.

Nearly a century later, the same attitude was behind the thought of J.M. Keynes. He was a rationalist, full of indignation at stupidity and prejudice, and confident that the management of the economy, as far as public policy goes, should be in the hands of the kind of highly intelligent civil servants that he had met in the India Office in his youth, and that an intellectual élite would be able to wear down prejudices in the electorate by rational argument. Against this, Marx drew attention to what was neglected in his day: the power of economic interest to influence judgments and create ideologies, which are perspectives within which evidence is selected and evaluated. Economic interest can, of course, be related to less comprehensive categories than that of class: for example, to the medical profession or clergy. Indeed the concept of class itself has been extensively examined and refined. Several recent documents from the World Council of Churches ignore this, and refer to 'the people' or 'people's power' or 'the masses' as if these terms refer to a uniform class; similarly 'the poor' are referred to without sufficient differentiation to make an adequate analysis of the contemporary scene possible.

Nevertheless, Marx launched a basic approach which we cannot escape: the source of the discipline known as the sociology of knowledge.[6] This is the study of the conditioning (*not* determining) factors involved in human knowing. It becomes clear that education of itself is no royal road to 'pure' judgments. Education can easily help us to more intelligent ways of pursuing ideological ends, but it may also help us to transcend conditioning factors. The latter should be our aim, even if we know that we can never totally succeed in jumping out of our skins into pure, unconditioned, social judgments.

We are more likely to be helped here by a commitment to a religion or philosophy which probes these deep issues. The Christian doctrine of original sin is a good key to understanding this aspect of our condition, while its doctrine of original righteousness is an encouragement to realize that there is something positive in us on which the indwelling presence of God's spirit can build if we live in the context of Christian community and worship. At any rate, we have to be post-Marxists, and allow for the force of economic interests in affecting judgments and policies. To ask 'Whose interests are being expressed?' is always a relevant question, but it is not necessarily a decisive one.

3. Marxist faith and Christian faith

How then are we to understand Marxism? Not as a science, but as a faith in the guise of a science, attracting to itself the prestige that is given to the natural sciences in the modern world together with the emotional force coming from a religious faith. To put it in another way, Marxism combines the scope of a metaphysic with the certainty of a natural science. Marx was of Jewish descent and shared in the Judaeo–Christian cultural heritage of biblical categories and images, blended with the deposit of Greek thought, which had been pervasive in Europe.

It is notable how many theological and biblical themes occur in a secular form in Marxist theory. To begin with, there is the antinomy which runs through Marxist thought that although the scientific theory provides a basis for forecasting what is certain to come in human history, there is nevertheless a strong moral challenge to embrace the workers' cause and speed the process, even though economic forces are inexorably working for moral ends. 'The wheel of history moves slowly to the ultimate but inevitable, irrepressible goal of history,'[7] is a quotation typical of much modern Marxism; another writer says that 'the stars in their courses are working for communism' (not realizing he is quoting from the book of Judges [5.20]).[8] This is very like the Old Testament prophets' view of God's relation to human history, especially that of Israel: for example, in the book of Isaiah the view taken of Assyria and Persia, or Jeremiah's view of Nebuchadnezzar as 'my servant' (27.6; 28.5). This raises questions in theological terms of providence and grace, of determinism and free will. One thinks of the classic controversy between Augustine and Pelagius, the former stressing pre-determining grace and the latter the freedom of the will; or in Marxism of the controversy between the more 'scientific' attitude of Marx and Engels, and Lenin's resolution to create the revolutionary situation by pushing the process on.

In Russia itself a more behaviourist attitude was adopted until about 1929; after that, with a series of five-year plans in operation, behaviourism lost favour. Once the decisive revolution had taken place in 1917, shortcomings could no longer be blamed plausibly on the social environment. St Paul expressed both sides of this issue in Philippians (2.13), where he urges Christians 'to work out your own salvation in fear and trembling, for it is God who works in you, inspiring both the will and the deed, for his chosen puposes'. It is doubtful whether Christian theology has ever got any further on this than St Paul.

Apart, however, from basic themes like these, there is a whole series of concepts in Marxism which are parallel to biblical ones.

1. *The Fall*: in Marxism it is the invention of private property, corrupting the idyll of primitive communism. How did it start? It is as inexplicable as the place of the serpent in the garden of Eden.

2. *The people of God*: the proletariat with its historical mission.

3. *The remnant of the people of God*: Lenin's differentiation of the class-conscious proletariat who can seize the opportunity from the *lumpen* proletariat, who are so submerged and depressed as to be incapable of effective action.

4. *The canon of scripture in the Bible*: the authorized texts of Marx, Engels and Lenin (Stalin was once in the canon, but has been cast out).

5. *The church*: the party, whose cell meetings have elements of praise, exposition, criticism and self-criticism, very like acts of worship.

6. *The reign of Christ for 1,000 years in Revelation 20*: the dictatorship of the proletariat.

7. *The new Jerusalem of Revelation 21 and 22*: the classless society, which brings us back again to the communism from which humanity started just as Revelation brings us back to the idyllic state of Eden in Genesis.

In so far as Marxism is a faith dressed in a scientific disguise, it is humane in intention, since it wants to remove alienation from humanity; but it is defective in its lack of an understanding of the human person. It also has a cruel view of history, since it is concerned for an ideal future in which those who have suffered and toiled in previous generations will have no part. That is all the more reason for Christians to honour those Marxists who have given their energies, and often their lives, for the cause of future generations of men and women, regardless of their lack of any part of it.

However, these wider aspects of Marxist doctrine and ethics are not our concern in this book. We are primarily concerned with economic issues, even though the two cannot be entirely separated. Those Christians who have recently made most use of Marxism have been the liberation theologians of Latin America: they have had a world-wide influence in the last twenty-five years. They have been clear that what they take of Marxism must be separated from its atheism. This at once presents a problem because, as I have mentioned, in its more 'scientific' claims (which these theologians tend to accept) Marxism hangs together, and its criticism of all religion is basic and cannot be separated from the rest. We have not considered it here, and I do not propose to do so, except to note that its view of religion is basically the same as its view of the state. Both have arisen as convenient weapons for ruling classes to oppress the ruled, so that in a classless society there will be no place for either, and religion will simply wither away. There will be no one with any reason to propagate it or to take refuge in believing it.[9]

The liberation theologians tend to say that Christians get their faith from the Bible and the doctrine which arises out of it, but that they need a 'science' to know what is going on today in order to act. That 'science' is Marxism. They take one further step and say that we shall only understand our Bible and our doctrine if we are first actively committed to the cause of the poor, otherwise we shall misunderstand it through a kind of 'false consciousness', to use a Marxist term, and produce a spurious other-worldly type of spirituality, which has been endemic in Christianity from its early centuries: precisely the kind of religion which Marx exposed. They have a strong case, though this is not the place to enlarge on it. If we grant the criticism, however, the point remains that without a reasonably competent understanding of what the current economic, social and political facts are, we could easily make bad mistakes in working for and with the poor instead of helping them. For while it is vital to listen *to* them (and most dominant classes and most churches most of the time have not been good at this), it does not follow that their interpretation of the wider context of what affects them is correct. It is because the liberation theologians realize this that they talk of the need for a 'science' to tell them. This itself shows the influence of Marxism. They do not examine the various Marxist theories; they assume them to be scientific. Clodovis Boff's doctoral thesis is an example.[10] He argues for three necessary steps: 1. The foundation in doctrine that Jesus sided with the poor; 2. Marxism is to be followed as a scientific understanding of society as against the alternative, a functional sociology, as exemplified in the work of Talcott Parsons;[11] 3. The development of political theology by applying a science of hermeneutics (that is to say how to interpret texts) to the Bible.

Boff's thesis was produced in 1976. There have been changes in the attitude of liberation theologians since then, partly under the pressure of events, partly in response to Vatican criticisms, some but not all of which are cogent,[12] and lately because of the collapse of the Soviet economies, about which Clodovis' brother Leonardo Boff made some glowing remarks as recently as 1987. Moreover Cuba, the only alternative economic model near them, is a dubious one. It has become clear that it is the biblical option for the poor, and the faith and spirituality derived from it, which is central to liberation theologians (and they are rather conservative biblical scholars), whilst there are fewer and fewer references to Marx in their writings.[13] It is evident that the Latin American economies are not examples of the classical free-enterprise economies; they are partly feudal and partly capitalist (70% of the arable land is owned by 2% of the population).

Latin American theologians have talked of socialism as an ideal, but never clearly defined it. But it is clear that they do not want anything like the command economy and the single-party role of the Soviet system; they want political democratic freedoms, but do not specify the structures and institutions which will realize the goal of social justice and at the same time secure these freedoms. Marxism is no help to them in their quest, and they are no help to us. But we need to take heed of their exposure of a false spirituality.[14]

The reason why Marxism is no help can be seen if we look at what has happened in Russia. The later history of Marxism, until the Chinese success, based on an agricultural and not an industrial proletariat, is largely bound up with the Russia of Lenin and Stalin. Lenin developed Marxist theory in *The State and Revolution* (1917), especially that of the class-conscious proletariat. Trotsky foresaw the danger of this vanguard turning into a party dictatorship, then into that of the Central Committee, and then into that of Stalin. But his own alternative was hopelessly utopian. As to the economic history of Russia since 1917, its startling progress from being an industrially backward country to being one with advanced technology has nothing to do with Marxist economics, which impeded it. Japan has made much more progress in this sense in the same period. The development took place in Russia because the irremovable government had the power to impose a scale of forced saving on the population which no government subject to a free election could have got away with. Consumers were systematically starved of goods. Now with a greater and more sophisticated urban population the whole economic system has broken down, together with the ideology which supported it.

4. Providence and history

To what conclusions does our survey of the Marxist response to capitalism lead? The most important one is that there are no 'scientific' laws of historical change, as is usually claimed by Marxists. The theories that Marx worked out can best be seen against the conditioning factors operating in the mid-nineteenth century. Those factors to which Marxism draws attention in criticizing all other social analyses also apply to its own. But I must emphasize again that conditioning does not mean determining. There was nothing inevitable about Marxism, and it must be allowed its elements of originality in its insights and in its errors. Once labourers and peasants all over the world, who have been pushed around and subjected to forces over which they had no control, have become 'conscientized' enough to take stock of their position and the possibility of exercising some influence in the hope of changing it, the insights of Marxism have spoken to them.[15] However, the Marxist analysis has not been sufficiently accurate to give an adequate diagnosis of what their situation is and the options for effective change.

Marxism has had an appeal among progressively-minded intellectuals in the 'West' because it has given them a secular reason for believing that history is working towards the realization of their ideals for humanity, taken from a Judaeo-Christian outlook whose basis they could no longer accept because in their view modern thought had made it incredible.[16]

There cannot be a 'science' of historical change in the way that some of the founding fathers of sociology, of which Marx was one, thought. The reactions of human beings are too indeterminate for that to be possible. For the same reason, there is no inevitable 'progress' in history. Christians may well believe that God's providence operates in his world in the sense that human structures and attitudes which flout his purposes for human well-being will not work and, sooner or later, will come to disaster. They may also well believe that God has not set limits to what humans may achieve if they stand by his purposes of love and justice. On the other hand, each generation has to win its own moral victories, and while a previous one can give its successor a good start, there is no guarantee that it will appropriate that start and not corrupt it. This is especially so because the most subtle corruptions of blind self-righteousness feed on virtues; vices are more easily recognized. There is no reason to believe that the rule of God, or kingdom of God, will ever be fully realized in human history; it calls in question all present achievements and is a challenge to reform them. This is a truly radical teaching, which it has been all too easy for churches to ignore, settling down with things as they are. It is one thing to exercise a reconciling and healing role in society; quite another to acquiese in structures of oppression. Rosemary Radford Ruether wisely says that there is no linear process in history, either revolutionary or evolutionary, leading to some salvation point. There was no paradise in the historical past and there is none in the historical future. Ethically, there is the ever-to-be-renewed and ongoing task of achieving a workable balance, free from 'the tyranny of impossible expectations'.[17]

In this connection it is unfortunate that some Christian theologians, rightly concerned with facing the Marxist phenomenon, have felt that it is necessary to parallel the Marxist utopian view of the historical process with a Christian one in terms of the apocalyptic writings in the Bible.[18] They draw on the language of a new heaven and a new earth, where God's historical purpose for humanity (and maybe nature too) will be fulfilled. They also say that the power of this future is to be experienced now in making decisions. It is, of course, true that we cannot be sure that these writings are not to be taken literally, nor can we be sure that Jesus will not literally return next year, or in the year 2000, however unlikely that may seem. But what is clear is that whilst we must always be alert to the new factors and not be tied to the past, alleged events in the future of which we have no knowledge now cannot be the basis of decision making. This is what was found to be case in New Testament times, when the expected imminent *parousia*, or return of Jesus, did not take place. Christians do believe in God's final triumph; they believe that the kingdom or rule of God inaugurated by the ministry of Jesus will be fulfilled – but not in the time and space we now experience. There are also movements in theology which confine God to the limits of our linguistic possibilities and whose horizon is therefore akin to that of Marx. They are a warning against over-confidence in the range of the theological claims we make, but they must not be allowed to obscure the reality of our glimpses of the transcendence of God.

These thoughts are in danger of taking us too far afield. In the area with which we are specially concerned, it follows that there is no inevitable breakdown of capitalism because of its inherent contradictions. It is proving very tough. Moreover, for many economic purposes no alternative to the market economy is on offer. Rather, it is the Marxist system, its economics and its ideology, which is in ruins. The truths which it stood for have now largely been absorbed into the mental background of this century. If not, they ought to be. We all need to be post-Marxists. But we no longer need to turn to particular Marxist analyses or the overall theory of Marxism to appropriate what we need to learn from them. No secure guidance is to be found there. So we turn to consider the main social and economic options that are available.[19]

5 The Triumph of Capitalism?

The collapse of the Soviet-style 'command' economies and the Marxist ideology going with them has been so spectacular that it has been easy for many people to say that this amounts to the triumph of capitalism in the long ideological war. However, the issue is not so simple, at the level of either ideology or practice.

It is difficult to quarrel with the ideology of Marxism in its concern to achieve a society based on the principle of 'from each according to his ability, to each according to his need', except perhaps to say that Marxism does not mention liberty.[1] In any case it is a utopia, and whether humans will ever overcome the problem of relatively scarce resources is very doubtful. If they do, whether they will voluntarily choose to distribute them in this way is even more doubtful. Meanwhile the theory of the Soviet-style economies, according to which they belong to the era of the dictatorship of the proletariat prior to the possibility of a communist society, is based on 'from each according to his work', which leaves a lot of questions to be asked, quite apart from the actual practice of those economies. Moreover, as we have seen, the understanding of the human person underlying the theory is seriously defective. There is little regard for the person because man – there is no sensitivity to feminism in Marxism – is a 'species being'; it is the collective that counts. Marxism has difficulty in coping with death. Even Stalin had to give way in the war of 1939–45 and allow the opening of churches to meet the demand for memorial services occasioned by the frightful loss of life among military and civilians. It is this defect which helped to allow the growth of centralized power and the failure to check its corruptions; all that the words 'Gulag Archipelago' conjure, or all that Arthur Koestler portrayed in his novel *Darkness at Noon*.[2]

In the ideology which has often gone with capitalism it is also the concept of the person which calls for criticism, as distinct from the idea of the market as such. Trouble arises when the market mechanism is erected into a philosophy of 'possessive individualism'.[3] We have seen that the market treats the factors of production, land, labour and capital alike, and in the case of labour this is to treat persons as things. There is no objection to this for a *part* of life, if it is set within a framework and context which expresses the reality that personhood is found in relationships: in the complexities of life many of the contacts between people are instrumental rather than relational. But the instrumental must be kept in place. The stress on the individual in the market must not turn into a philosophy of individualism.

Sometimes talk of personal responsibility in Christian circles amounts to this. Many Christians have a horror of being dependent on others; and even if they give, they find it hard to receive, gracefully. They do not see that we are bound together in the bonds of our common humanity, in relations of giving and receiving in our personal lives and on a communal basis. 'Persons-in-relation' is an understanding fundamental to the Christian faith, though one does not have to be a Christian to accept it.[4] Individuals are replaceable; each person is unique. And persons must accept responsibility for leading their own lives; no one else can do this for them. They must make their own conscientious decisions.

Most of the Christian social and socialist critiques of capitalism have been misplaced. But that does not mean that capitalism has triumphed in any unambiguous sense. Apart from the mistaken philosophy of *laisser-faire*, it has many practical defects, to which I shall return. Meanwhile we can note that one way of expressing criteria which Christians might bring to the social order is the liberty, equality and fraternity of the French Revolution. There it came in a secular setting, but it was in reality the heir of European civilization with its Judaeo-Christian roots. Capitalism stresses liberty, and socalism equality for the sake of fraternity. Many capitalists also want to allow for fraternity, but only by individual choice. Socialists want to organize it. It is dangerous to pursue any one of the three without reference to the others. The task is to find at any given time the best mix of the three, in order to maximize the possibilities of human fulfilment.

Capitalism has triumphed in so far as the market mechanism is seen as having a key role in the economy. But pure *laisser-faire* and the total command economies are not the alternatives. The first is not practised even where it is most advocated;[5] the second is in ruins. We are about to consider the social market and the democratic socialist models, after looking more closely at the problems created by the breakdown of the command economies. The question is where the stress is to be laid at a given time: towards liberty or towards equality in the interests of fraternity. We need to get beyond the rhetoric that portrays what is individual as good and what is state-run as bad. This has been the tone of powerful voices in the 1980s. But there is evidence that it has not carried general conviction.[6]

Another way of putting this is to say that a market using the incentives of competition and profit is a useful human device, but one which requires a firm framework to prevent abuses and ensure a proper status for each citizen. There must be as much competition as possible (to achieve efficiency in the economic sense), and as much control and planning as necessary (to avoid abuses and remedy deficiencies) in the market system. This will involve at least four requirements:

1. *Harnessing self-interest to the common good.* An example is the control of pollution. Almost all human activity involves pollution, but pollution must not get out of bounds. One way of controlling it is by regulation involving inspectors, and court cases in the case of infringements. Another way is to use the price mechanism, allowing competitive bidding for the rights to pollute up to the limit thought advisable. There is likely to be a place for both methods, but the second is the less cumbersome.

2. *Providing a strong welfare state.* This will involve citizen rights and responsibilities: helping them to adjust to market changes without undue hardship, as well as providing mutual support in the incidental hazards of life, including those endemic at particular stages, like infancy, childhood and old age.

3. *Ensuring that private centres of economic power do not become more powerful than the government*: Here a careful watch on trans-national corporations is specially needed, together with the decentralization of all that it is not imperative to deal with centrally into intermediate bodies, in order to prevent too much power resting in one place.

4. *Taking participation in decision-making seriously in matters where vital interests of citizens are at stake*: At a low level everyone may be

able to participate directly; but mostly forms of indirect representation have to be devised.

These are some of the questions that the USSR and Eastern European countries are having to face. Let us look at them.

1. Dismantling the legacy of Marxist economics

There is no parallel to draw upon. Even China's agrarian reform in the 1980s is not comparable. The attitude varies in different states. The USSR was being timid and Poland bold. This is a task of enormous importance. Failure could easily lead to the kind of populist authoritarian governments which are common in Latin America. The problem is, as we have seen, that the command economy is not an attempt to mimic the market system (though Oscar Lange attempted to show how that could be done),[7] but one in which producers are told what to produce and how much to charge for it, and these prices are not market signals but fixed arbitrarily by planners. One of Mikhail Gorbachev's leading economic advisers in 1988 wanted producers to compete for customers, discover what they wanted, find suppliers and then produce the desired goods as profitably as possible, avoiding waste.[8] However, with the state still owning the factors of production, producers cannot know the economic costs of production and therefore cost what they themselves produce. That is why Gorbachev's law encouraging co-operative enterprises had little effect, because these enterprises have had trouble in finding raw materials, since the state has had control of the wholesale trade. The policy does work better, however, in the case of non-manufacturing enterprises, like hairdressing and restaurants.

Gorbachev had to go further. Decentralizing a command economy is not enough. Planners and managers do not like even this. It suddenly thrusts them into a bracing position of which they have had no experience. Again, if prices are freed there is danger of vast inflation because of the amount of purchasing power accumulated by Soviet citizens who have so little available on which to spend it. The crucial question is, will economically inefficient enterprises be allowed to go bust? Is there a real role for the entrepreneur, the risk-taker? Some ask whether you can have capitalism without capitalists, but a better way of putting it is: can you have a market without entrepreneurs? The answer is, no. What is done with profits, and how those stricken by losses can be helped to make a new start, are different questions.

A real market needs to be created. Ovbiously, when almost everything has been controlled, this means a vast increase in the private sector (it might be wise to *give* shares in state assets to groups of citizens), combined with stricter controls on the public sector, in the interests of economic efficiency, so that much of it shrinks, especially in heavy industries. This means creating unemployment, and embarking on job re-training schemes, together with a social safety net for displaced workers. It means letting very many prices find their own level, and working towards a convertible currency. All this of course also applies to Eastern European countries in their somewhat varying, but basically similar, economies.

In this task they all need well-thought-out help from the 'West'. As with the Third World, trade is as important as aid, and imports from the East must not be stifled by protectionist policies in the European Community. Indeed, it would be wise to incorporate the Eastern countries into the Common Market as soon as possible. In addition, they need grants and loans to build up their foreign reserves, and to make to small and medium firms if they will put up some risk capital themselves. Furthermore their debts to Western governments and banks should be cancelled. Let us remember the wisdom of J.M.Keynes after the 1914–18 war in criticizing the efforts to squeeze Germany economically, and the disastrous effect this had in contributing to the rise of Hitler. If we stand aside and let the USSR and the other Eastern European countries struggle to sort themselves out without help, they will be financially crippled, and the economic misery that results could have similar serious, even frightening, political results.

Meanwhile in Western Europe there are two economic orders which are neither *laisser-faire* nor Soviet style.

2. The social market economy

This is often called capitalism with a human face, and that is not surprising, for the European roots whence it came lie deep in the Roman Catholic tradition of social theology as it was renewed by the encyclical *Rerum Novarum* (1891). The encyclical had a stress on the human, the personal, which lies deep in a Christian understanding of the world.

Social market economies are linked with Christian Democratic parties in Western Europe. They are found in Austria, Belgium, Holland, Italy, Luxembourg, Switzerland and what was West Germany until the re-unification of the two Germanies. Britain is missing. For just as the British Labour party has different roots from continental socialist parties, so has the British Conservative Party from continental Christian Democratic parties. Religious factors largely account for the difference in both cases. Here we are not concerned with the Labour Party, but with the difference between Liberals and Conservatives in Britain and those on the mainland European continent. The continental roots lie in quarrels between clerical and lay parties in the nineteenth century. Roman Catholic social theology before 1891 was fossilized, fixed in the assumptions of a bygone era, which the blank opposition of the Church to the French Revolution had made even more fixed. Pius IX's famous *Syllabus of Errors* (1864) condemned most of the movements for change as industrial society developed. The church was locked into the presuppostions of the traditional Christendom situation in which church and state were integrated. Lay parties tended to be against control by clerics and to want a separation of church and state. Clerics thought that political democracy was the road to atheism. But it was only after the 1914–18 war that the situation crystallized politically, when Dom Luigi Sturzo, a Roman Catholic priest, founded in Italy Europe's first Christian Democratic party in 1919. His aim was to ally Roman Catholicism with democracy, but not in a church-run party, and to stand for social reforms now implicit in church social teaching. Similar parties soon followed in Europe and, indeed, in Latin America.[9] Sturzo was driven into exile by the Fascists in 1924. However, an international group developed in Paris which came into its own after the 1939–45 war. It included Alcide de Gasperi from Italy, Robert Schumann from France and Konrad Adenauer from Germany. From them came the inspiration for the Common Market, beginning with the Coal and Steel Community and, beyond that, thoughts of European integration, not least to heal the national divisions which from Europe, the heartland of Christendom, had plunged the world into two disastrous wars in this century. They were heirs of

Rerum Novarum, and heralds of the Second Vatican Council twenty years later.

They were consciously seeking a third way between what they saw as liberal capitalist individualism and socialist collectivism. The term personalism was congenial to them, influenced by the social philosophy of Jacques Maritain, the French neo-Thomist, who was widely read at the time.[10] Maritain explored the richness and corporateness of the term person as applied to the human being, compared with the thinness and separateness of the term individual. This led those influenced by him to stress the building of political responsibility upwards from the grass roots rather than downwards from a centralized authority, an idea which was to be expressed in the encyclical *Quadragesimo Anno* in 1931, which introduced the term 'subsidiarity' to Christian social theology. Inclined to minimize endemic social conflicts, as church teaching often does, the encyclical talked of solidarity among all sections of society. Most Christian Democratic parties had quite strong trade union sections, though West Germany did not. These sections were suspect by secular unions, as weakening working-class solidarity and liable to give way under pressure in a conflict with management. The stress on social solidarity also slid rather easily into support for Mussolini's specious 'corporate state', which *Quadragesimo Anno* was widely interpreted as favouring.

Economics was not a strong point in the Christian Democratic outlook. But, ironically, it was a Protestant member of the West German Christian Democratic Union (which has many Protestant members), Ludwig Erhard, who was the architect of the social market economy, or the free market with a social conscience, which has been behind the great strength of the German economy ever since. For the rest, there are different strains within Christian Democratic parties, as in almost all parties. In Germany, for example, the Bavarian party is more nationalist. More seriously, these parties seem to have lost their way. Vatican social theology has become more critical of 'Western' economies, as encyclicals like *Populorum Progressio* (1967), *Laborem Exercens* (1981) and *Sollicitudo Rei Socialis* (1988) bear witness. It would call for a more radical social market economy than the Christian Democratic parties have envisaged, and it could also work with a democratic socialist economy (which we have yet to consider), so that the term socialism can no longer occasion the blank opposition it did in papal teaching in 1891 and after.

In France, Giscard d'Estaing is now the heir of the earlier Christian Democratic position, whilst the leaders in the movement for a more integrated Europe are Jacques Delors (who is a Roman Catholic, but does not operate directly from any confessional basis) and the more secular François Mitterand. In Italy the Christian Democrats lost the referenda on divorce and abortion in 1974 and 1981, and in the 1984 Euro-elections fell behind the Communists in votes. Christian Democratic leaders like Lubbers, Marten, Andreotti and Kohl seem like political 'fixers', concerned with staying in power, but not to have had any new ideas for decades. They differ in that the West Germans still seem to see socialism as the enemy, whilst in Italy, Belgium and Holland they are used to working with socialists. They are not, however, free marketeers.

At a European level the Christian Democrats are known as the European People's Party. The British Conservative Euro-MPs have tried to join it, but so far have not been admitted because, whatever their own opinions may be, they have been tarred with Mrs Thatcher's opposition to what the European People's Party favours: a monetary union, the EC Social Charter, more power to the European Parliament, and a common foreign and security policy. In contrast, the Greek New Democracy Party, the Irish Fine Gael and the Spanish People's Party have been admitted. Things may change now that Mrs Thatcher has gone, but at present the British Tories are organizationally isolated from the mainstream of European Christian Democratic politics. It remains to be seen how this mainstream will propose policies which combine a relative freedom for the market with 1. less of the distortion produced at present by the huge subsidies to farmers through the Common Agricultural Policy (and the extent of protectionism it imposes against imports from the Third World); 2. social policies which establish through taxation the substance of a welfare state; and 3. the strengthening of union power in relation to management which is adumbrated in the Social Charter.

3. The democratic socialist economy

The socialist stress is on equality (legal, political, social and economic) for the sake of fraternity. This is not to ignore liberty, but to argue that in order to exercise liberty effectively a citizen needs a certain level of income, health care, social services and education. This runs contrary to the assertion of Hayek and others that the term injustice should be confined to the restriction of liberty by deliberate action, since the term *social* justice has no meaning. Social market and democratic socialist positions are committed both to market and to non-market institutions, to efficiency in the economic sense in wealth creation and to re-distributive social policies and institutions.[11] The difference is in the thrust of social policies because of the socialist stress on the criterion of equality.

This at once raises the question of differentials. Another way of putting it is the need for a theory of legitimate inequality which carries public consensus. Still another way is to ask how much economic rent is needed to mobilize the ability of those who are endowed with more of it than most. The financial rewards and increments which the upper levels of management have been giving themselves in recent years are inordinate and scandalous to socialists, and not only to them. Related to this is how to handle the trio of unemployment, inflation and free collective bargaining, which all market societies face.

In liberal democracies electorates want all three: freedom from inflation, full employment and freedom to bargain over wages and salaries. They are all connected, and cannot be achieved simultaneously. To return to the example of unemployment, referred to in Chapter 2, full employment (which is to allow for up to 3–4% to be out of work for a short spell as they change jobs) and free collective bargaining together lead to inflation, because the increased wages secured will outpace increased productivity. More money will chase much the same available stock of goods and services. Moreover, if the inflation is expected to continue, wage claims will anticipate this, and leap-frogging settlements will make the inflation worse.[12] Some unemployment is a necessity in a dynamic and changing economy. It must play a part in government strategy.

There is rarely the courage to admit this. Social policy needs to cushion the effect of unemployment and promote the transfer from one job to another. The more successful a full employment policy is, the more some form of incomes policy is necessary. Politically such a policy is hard to implement and messy, but no more messy than an unregulated market economy. It is not popular among the 90% or so who are not unemployed and not likely to be, and it is not popular with Labour Party supporters and with trade unions. The attachment of unions to unfettered collective bargaining is appropriate in a *laisser-faire* economy, but not in a social market or democratic specialist one. Without some incomes policy the young and the unskilled will be hard done by, partly because of the 'last in, first out' system when jobs are cut; whilst an effort to create a reasonable minimum wage (in terms of the standard of living it permits) will be nullified by the effort of those better paid to maintain their previous differentials over the lower paid. Governments need to sponsor rapid retraining of those with obsolete skills, who are made redundant, in skills which are required, and at the same time greatly expand and pay for the personal services of the unskilled.[13]

Sweden is the only example of an advanced industrial economy which is democratic socialist, so it is important to pay some attention to it. Sweden has had the highest taxes of any industrial country, the most generous welfare state, with excellent social services, the narrowest wage differentials (lower than the Soviet Union) and the biggest percentage of trade union membership.[14] The high level of taxation has meant less personal income to dispose of as one wishes, much lower than in most countries in Western Europe, but there has been very little backlash against this. High taxes have been considered a price worth paying for the services provided. During 1990 inflation rose from 7% to 11.5%, whilst unemployment was only $1\frac{1}{2}$%. There is an active labour market policy designed to move workers from declining to expanding industries by retraining schemes and relocation grants. Unemployment benefit is paid for 300 days, and anyone who refuses to take a job or to be retrained will have it stopped after that. Only 8% of the unemployed have been out of a job for more than a year, a much lower proportion than in the European Community. Market forces decide whether firms in manufacturing thrive or fail, whilst wage bargaining is decided for the most part by centralized bargaining according to what it is agreed the economy can afford.

What are the snags? The economy is clearly overheated with only $1\frac{1}{2}$% unemployed. If it is to be efficient in the economic sense it needs at least 3% unemployed and, after recent inflationary pressures, the government in 1991 has been proposing to make that something of a target by cutting public expenditure. Is the Swedish economy becoming sluggish and uncompetitive? Will it be able to continue to pay for its welfare state? Half its exports go to the European Community. It does not look as if will stay outside that much longer. If it enters, will it have less freedom in industry (some shares carry no voting rights, to prevent foreigners owning Swedish industry: the EC will not allow this)? Sweden's well-established industries – steel, paper and heavy engineering – are technically advanced, but is the economy sufficiently innovative? The public sector unions cover just over one-third of the work force and are very powerful. They are also more shielded from international competition, and so big pay rises do not necessarily price them out of jobs. Similarly, generous sick pay means that the rate of absenteeism is double that of the EC. (This, of course, may be both more humane and lead to no less production in the long run.)

So far the Social Democrats, who have been in power most of the time since 1945, and the non-socialist parties, who were in power from 1976–82, have pursued much the same policies, which could be said to be politically the easy way out: subsidize loss-making industries and increase public expenditure, especially when more than half the electorate depends on the public sector as employers, employees or pensioners. So there are snags.

There are always snags. There is no type of economy which does not produce them. In terms of quality of life, attitude to immigrants, and a concern for the Third World, Sweden has the best record of the highly-industrialized and technologically-advanced economies. To raise questions about the parameters within which it can move is not to suggest that it cannot tolerably resolve its problems at least as well as, and perhaps better than, other countries who are similarly advanced.

A widespread public consensus on wage policy is essential if unemployment is to be kept not to the unrealistic $1\frac{1}{2}\%$, but to 3% or 4%. Here there are signs of strain. Centralized pay bargaining means that the Trade Union Confederation and the Employers' Federation must agree annually on a notional norm, taking into account the international situation. In the 1970s some trade unions broke away in order to get either a higher low-pay wage *or* a bigger differential. In the 1990s some employers want decentralized pay bargaining, relating wages more directly to productivity. These are more *laisser-faire* aims. If these are what many Swedes do want, they will have moved to a more social-market economy. They cannot have it with the more democratic, egalitarian society they have had in recent decades.

4. The market as a servant of human purposes

Markets are useful for risk-taking innovation. There is a major role for competition and the entrepreneur. But there is no case for saying that markets work best if they are left alone. That is to erect a false social philosophy on the concept of the market. Much thought, therefore, needs to be given to the social framework within which markets operate. Can they not serve more egalitarian ends? Can they be more radical than Sweden? In addition to the role of the capitalist, is it not possible also to have markets without capitalists? Many think not; and the latest of Hayek's many books returns to this theme.[15] Is it not possible to have indicative planning but not the centralized command economies of the Soviet style? This question was much discussed decades ago, but has been submerged since under the rhetoric of the New Right. It needs to be re-addressed.[16] For we cannot do without markets, nor can we make do with them alone. To recapitulate, other things being equal, markets are a highly efficient way of getting economic decisions made in accordance with the freedom of choice expressed by consumers: that is, by the dispersed exercise of political and economic power. They are an incentive to thrift and innovation, so tending to maximize the productivity of relatively scarce economic resources. On the other hand, left to themselves market economies produce cumulative inequalities of income which distort the market by drawing the relatively scarce resources to what the wealthy want and away from the necessities of the poor; they cannot provide what we call public goods, and they are bad at dealing with externalities. They have to be rigorously monitored to prevent the creation of cartels, quotas, monopolies and other restrictions, and to question those whose vested interest actively campaigns for them. Regulation of trade union operations and disciplines is also needed. Moreover while markets give play to a proper profit motive, greed and the chicanery it occasions are just round the corner, and powerful vigilance is required to keep them in check. Scandals in Britain, the

USA and Japan have made this abundantly clear. A market economy needs strong state regulation. Voluntary codes of ethics and of good practice are also important adjuncts to regulation. Effectively self-policing of markets is better than government regulation, but it is not enough. Both types of control are needed.

In matters of production there are many ways of blurring a clear-cut distinction between owners, managers and the work-force.[17] As far as ultimate control of private corporations is concerned, the responsibilities of corporate shareholders – insurance companies, unit trusts, and pension funds – need to be taken much more seriously.

Small shareholders can do something by checking their investment against criteria such as those of the Ethical Investment Movement and, occasionally and with great difficulty, can produce an organized campaign on some issue for the annual meeting of the corporation. But this can only be sporadic and occasional. The main weight must rest with the institutional shareholders.

As far as the distribution of wealth is concerned, a positive attitude to taxation is needed among citizens. It is a good thing to pay taxes! And also to be alert that they are well spent. A strong infrastructure in the essential services of health, education, housing, personal social services and pensions is needed. The physical structure of the country, especially in the urban areas, and its communications need to be cared for. There is no reason why all these should not work in an egalitarian direction, and all be related to a politically free society. In it there will be vigorous public discussion, and the various special interests will state their case in the public forum. Freedom of information will be regarded as a priority. To end this list I note that an integrated system of taxation and benefits instead of the present mish-mash should be worked for. At present tax allowances and social benefits are uncoordinated, so that it is possible that a greater income from work than from social security can lead to a loss of net income through lack of entitlement to benefits. All this is the catalogue of a current agenda. It is much more to the point than a polarization of capitalism versus a discredited Soviet-style socialism.

Lively differences of opinion over its various items will not be surprising, some favouring more of a social market and some a more market socialist scale of priorities. Church statements and individual Christians need to be engaged in these debates, bringing what theological light on them they have to offer. It is not to be expected that they will arrive at agreed detailed conclusions, but they may be able to throw more light on the questions. In the next chapter we shall consider some recent Christian contributions to current issues in the economic order.

6 The Economic Order in Recent Christian Thought

1. Protestant spirituality and the New Right

It is remarkable how little articulate Christian opinion has supported the ideology of the 'New Right'. There is hardly anything equivalent to the Christian political economy of 1798–1833.[1] The New Right has two characteristics. The first is an onslaught on the inefficiencies and corruptions of the actions of the state in the economic order, contrasted with an ideal picture of the working of the market, as if it were a practical possibility, and as if in practice it did not also have its flaws and deficiencies. In as far as any are admitted, it is said, much on the lines of Hayek's arguments, that they are less serious and less hard to correct than the failure of government 'interference' in markets. This spills over into the second characteristic, a defence of invidualism, associated with political and economic liberty as an overall philosophy or ideology, using the term 'ideology' in the broad sense of what holds human beings together in the social order. Adherents of the New Right are the foremost modern utopians now that Marxist utopianism has disintegrated. Even when it has followed the first characteristic of the New Right, articulate Christian opinion has not usually been willing to follow the second.

Yet the second characteristic is in fact deeply rooted in less articulate forms of Protestant Christianity as it has been inherited in the predominantly Protestant culture of the United Kingdom.[2] This attitude is shown in a diluted secular form in the unreflective attitudes of many ordinary citizens in the 'Clapham Omnibus', and also in those of many in the pews on a Sunday. It instinctively thinks of the individual as primary and of social relations as a secondary and to some extent optional addition. Grumbling about taxation is endemic to it. I experienced this in those among whom I grew up, and it has spread to the more skilled working-class families who have become upwardly mobile as a result of the rise in the standard of living in the last generation. A significant number of these had moved from Labour to Conservative by the General Election of 1987. Like many of us, at least some of the time, they can hold inconsistent opinions. They can like the scale and type of social benefits now associated with a welfare state and at the same time complain about, and exaggerate, the weight of taxation needed to pay for them. It is significant that the phrase 'the taxpayers' money' is so powerful a phrase in Tory rhetoric that it is now being used by the Labour party. Yet a moment's reflection shows the unreality of the idea latent in the phrase, that the individual, or family 'man', has earned his or her income by individual efforts, independently of social processes which have nurtured and surrounded them, so that a very special reason is needed to justify the state taking any of it away by taxation.

The Protestant spirituality behind this attitude (often inconsistently combined in the modern world with srong nationalist sentiments, but that is another story) is a stress on personal responsibility and a horror of dependency. There is an important half-truth here, as we have seen, which without the other half becomes a serious distortion. The importance of Mrs Thatcher was that she is a product of this kind of Protestant spirituality and articulates it. She must have been the most forceful Christian Prime Minister since Gladstone in her personal beliefs. Her attitude was most revealingly expressed in an interview to a women's magazine[3] in which she said, '... there is no such thing as society. There are individual men and women, and there are families. And no government can do anything except through people and people look to themselves first.' She went on to say that one must *first* (my italics) meet an obligation before one has an entitlement. Several of those who generally support her, thinking it is absurd to deny the reality of society, have said that in context she did not really mean this, and in the chapter in which he quotes the remark Brian Griffiths says the same, but the text itself makes the excuses unconvincing.

This remains a valuable example of a common attitude among churchgoers, and is greatly at variance with most recent articulate

Christian reflection. It turns the Christian gospel on its head. It says that one must *first* earn merit (meet an obligation) before being accepted (have an entitlement). The Christian faith, however, is that God's graciousness is such that it is not rare, and to be earned by effort, but constant, overflowing and free; it is to be accepted first, and then to be followed by a life of joyous response. The graciousness is shown in creation, for instance in that rain falls and the sun shines upon all alike, and in the re-creation inaugurated by the teaching and actions of Jesus. It has been hard enough for the Christian church itself to act on this, for we all tend to want to earn our acceptance by God rather than to admit that we cannot do this and must learn to receive before we can give; and it would be folly to suppose that the state could embody this fully in its institutions, or even do so as well as a church can. But the strength of the welfare state is that it does acknowledge a status of the citizen first; it does not start by discriminating between deserving and undeserving citizens.

True, the welfare state will not be able to follow the inexhaustible patience of God, yearning for a joyous response and not giving up when it fails to win it, even to four hundred and ninety times; but it will maintain this affirmation of a citizen's status from infancy to old age. In this it reflects the facts of human life. As we have seen, the structures of human life in family, work, political authority and culture, surround us and bear down upon us from pregnancy and infancy onwards to old age. The structures vary enormously in their empirical features, and can range from the benevolent to the tyrannous, but they are always there. The fact that we can at least partially transcend them, and should try to use what influence we possess in society to improve them, witnesses to the truth in the stress on personal responsibility. But this follows from our status as citizens and does not require us to earn an entitlement first.[4]

It is worth pausing to reflect how deep the individualism goes in Christian circles by referring to the call to the nation by the Archbishops of Canterbury and York in 1975 which marked the beginning of Donald Coggan's time as Archbishop of Canterbury. It asked two questions: 'What sort of society do we want?', and 'What sort of people do we need to be in order to achieve it?' It omitted a third question: 'What sort of social structures do we need to help the formation of people to be what we need them to be?' I do not remember any comment on this omission at the time. It is easy to understand that. Concentration on the first two leaves the issue at the level of personal attitudes, so the churches can concentrate on 'changing lives'. Bringing in the third, and referring to structures, involves 'politics' in a wide sense; it involves 'changing structures'. Here the churches are afraid of controversy and disagreement among their members, and disruption of Christian fellowship. Yet politics is a sea in which we must all swim. For to be non-political, or apolitical, is itself a political stance; it tacitly supports the *status quo*, and does so irresponsibly by lack of attention rather than conscientious decision. Churches may try to salve their conscience by urging their individual members to be concerned politically, but as corporate bodies they cannot avoid politics. The task for them as churches is to handle the issues appropriately. I shall have more to say about this in the next chapter. Meanwhile I must stress that it is a serious deformation of the Christian faith to assume that it is concerned with changing persons and not also with changing structures.

2. Brian Griffiths

Brian Griffiths, formerly Dean of the City University (London) Business School and later head of Mrs Thatcher's Policy Unit in 10 Downing Street, not surprisingly defends the economic policies of her government,[5] but he does not share the ideology of the New Right and is an advocate of a social market economy. He makes the standard New Right apologia for the market and criticisms of the inefficiency of public enterprises, and of the dependency created by the redistributive policies of a welfare state. But he is quite clear that the free market is not 'natural', nor an expression of a law of God, but a human device. He does not see labour as an inert factor of production. He is opposed to the philosophy of possessive individualism which has gone with capitalism, and he does not think that social justice is a meaningless concept, but favours distributive justice. He thinks that human problems are basically 'spiritual'. He sees that capitalism needs a firm moral foundation to underpin its market sysem, and thinks that Christian commitment is really necessary if it is to work.

This is too simple a view in the plural society and interlocked world in which we are placed. We must rid ourselves of any hint that one has to be a Christian in order to have sound moral commitments. It is necessary to seek and foster the best elements common to the major religions and ideologies if the world is to hold together in a tolerable form. That is what the traditional and often misunderstood natural law concept is about. It is concerned with elucidating a *moral* 'law', a recognition of which is implied in our very concept of what it is to be a human being and not a species less than human. To some extent that must underlie the success of capitalism in such areas as Japan and South-East Asia.

The individualistic side of Griffiths' Protestantism is shown when he says that the kingdom of God in Jesus' teaching is a challenge addressed to indivduals (as Simon and Andrew are called from their fishing). He does not stress that all who respond become members of a people of God, so that, as Paul says in his letter to the Romans (12.5), 'We who are united with Christ, though many, form one body, and belong to one another as its limbs and organs.'

Griffiths urges us to start with the individual, not the collective, though this could equally well be put the other way round, so long as both are pursued. He would not disagree with the pursuit of both. But starting with the individual the furthest he can go is to ask unrealistically for a *simultaneous* change of values in both individual and collective. He can see that the nature of the family can influence personal values, but he does not carry this over into the structures of work and political authority and see that in their structure changes can also have a *prior* influence on personal values and, in Bernard Bosanquet's phrase in reference to the task of the state, 'hinder hindrances to the good life'. One of the most obvious examples is the attitude to crime fostered in the substructures inhabited by the marginalized inhabitants of deprived inner-city and housing-estate areas of the United Kingdom. They constitute nearly one-fifth of the population. What in other areas is seen as dubiously deviant behaviour is there taken as normal.

Griffiths sees the social-market economy as capitalism with a Christian basis; he does not claim that it is the only economic expression of the Christian faith, but that it is compatible with that faith. In the spectrum of opinion in the Conservative party there are many who would agree, as do nearly all the other Conservatives in the European Parliament with their Christian roots. That is why on the whole they support the proposed Social Charter, which covers such matters as the free movement of workers; the improvement of working conditions; the right to strike; equitable treatment for part-time and temporary workers; collective bargaining; and the right of workers to information, consultation and some participation in the decision-making structures in industry. It is to these that Mrs Thatcher's kind of British Conservative is opposed, and it is their attitude which finds scarcely any support in recent articulate Christian thinking. I now consider further examples of this thinking. It will be seen that each raises problems of its own.

3. The Commission on the Churches' Participation in Development

Reflection on economic issues in the World Council of Churches has been mainly in the hands of the Commission on the Churches' Participation in Development (CCPD) which was formed in 1970. It has had an Advisory Group on Economic Matters since 1979 which has issued five reports; these were gathered together into one book.[6] The World Council of Churches has many advantages in bringing together Christians on a global basis for mutual reflection, including representatives of groups and peoples who often never get a hearing otherwise. It encounters a problem in that it is hard for meetings to achieve a real sharing and understanding in the limited time available, and expense restricts their frequency. The results are liable to be a bit rough and ready. One would hope that an advisory group on a special topic might have found things easier, but the economics group does not seem to have done. Its report varies a lot in quality and does not always cohere within itself. However, its basic supposition is right in explicitly differentiating political economy from economics. So are its aims for the churches, which are three. It highlights:

1. The need to identify the main directions of change required. It is generally better for churches to keep at this middle level of main directions than to go into detailed policies, because the more detailed one becomes, the more likelihood there is of genuine differences of opinion in interpreting such data as are available, and on the probable outcome of the different policies that are on offer. However, even this middle level requires adequate tools for analysing the current evidence as best we can, allowing for human limitations and ideological perspectives; little is said about this.

2. The need to identify some of the valid means for achieving at least part of these desirable changes.

3. The need to test the operation of churches and church-related organizations in the relevant areas by the standards they propose to others. This is a very important aim. Churches are prone to think that they can issue disinterested advice to all and sundry as if they were above the problems to which they refer, whereas in many ways they are part of these problems, in the way they handle their property and liquid financial resources, and how they relate to their own personnel and those of other bodies with whom they deal.

In this CCPD report the best discussion is of the international financial system, involving the International Monetary Fund, the World Bank and GATT (the General Agreement on Trade and Tariffs), all stemming from the Bretton Woods Agreement of 1945, under which the world economy flourished until 1971, when dollar-gold convertibility was suspended. Without going into its survey in detail, one can say that it sets out the general situation well and comes to the conclusion that in this area decisions cannot be taken by the general public, such as an electorate, because they are too technical.

Here is an issue that needs some discussion: the role of the technical in decision-making. In this case it is in the economic sphere. It could be some other sphere, as for instance the medical. Decisions cannot be made solely on the basis of technical specialized knowledge in either case, but they cannot be made without it. I would not easily admit that even in monetary matters decisions can be made only by experts; the task is to express them in a way which makes public discussion sensible. It is a pity the CCPD did not reflect on this problem. How do we cope with experts, especially when they differ, as they often do? How do we test whether experts are remaining within their expertise or moving beyond it? And whether they have some acknowledged or unrealized intellectual or personal vested interest which affects their judgment? These issues need looking into. But it is important for the role of expertise to be accepted. In a good deal of ecumenical literature in recent years, expertise has been regarded with suspicion as élitism, as distinct from listening to, and siding at the grass roots with, the poor and marginalized. Yet without the element of expertise one is quite likely to hinder the cause of these groups by adopting mistaken policies rather than to help it.

The rest of this CCPD document is less tightly written. The background is the failure of the new international economic order urged by the United Nations, and the mixture of affluence and misery which characterizes the present one. How do we arrive at a more just order, and one sustainable for future generations? I shall refer to this again in the last chapter. For the present, the point I want to stress is that the document does not come closely to grips with the basic economic problems we have already discussed; and when it comes to the realm of political economy it is apt to blur the distinction between this and economics, and also to propose an idealistic programme which totally reverses the ills to which attention has been drawn, as if it were a possibility achievable by decisions made today.

It calls for a new paradigm with people at the centre of the economic system, in the sense that they should participate at all levels in the social control of the major productive sectors of the economy, and for peoples' values, not private profit for the few, to animate the whole. This applies particularly to the poor, to women, and to minority groups, for the poorest and most oppressed must *direct* (my italics) the processes of decision-making so that authoritarian structures can be overcome. Economic growth and technical modernization are viewed with suspicion. Indeed the document quotes with approval the view of many Christians that the market system needs to be transformed if a holistic human society is to emerge. The insecurity, selfishness and inequality inherent in the free market mechanism must be overcome, not by reinforcing the present order, nor by organizing for change around long-term complementary self-interest (as the Brundtland report urged),[7] but because self-interest is incompatible with the gospel. Instead, a just, participatory and sustainable society 'according to the gospel message' must be organized.

Lastly, apart from raising necessary questions about the accountability of trans-national corporations, the document wants them de-linked from the international economy, and shows a general suspicion of international trade, reminiscent of the old mercantilism. Self-reliance is advocated for nations so that they are not vulnerable to the decisions of others (whose economic and political power may be much greater than their own); autonomous and self-sustaining development should be the aim. The report is consistent on this position, for it urges the developed countries also to be self-reliant, and not dependent on the natural resources or food supplies of developing countries.

There are other tendencies in this CCPD report which are not consistent with its main drift. For instance, at one point self-reliance is advocated in order not to be *completely* dependent on the decisions of others, which is a considerable modification. I shall not mention further inconsistencies, because I hope that the previous chapters of the present book will enable the reader to disentangle the confusions in this report, and to realize that for the most part it is of little use in furthering noble aims which most Christians would surely accept. One would expect better from an advisory group on economic matters.

Much the same is true of another CCPD publication, *Economics: a Matter of Faith*, but in this case there is more excuse, for it is really a cry of distress from the marginalized[8] as they experience the present economic order, rather than any worked-out alternative. It says that the present economic system challenges the core of the Christian faith in various respects, beginning with the oppression and starvation of millions. It goes on to say that we must reject the ideology of the market (which I also have urged), but not the market itself (which I have also urged). However, then comes the old error about finance ('so long as it doesn't multiply money for money's sake'). Hostility is expressed to a system which relies upon earning interest (and though churches cannot free themselves from it, they can take symbolic action against it). The alternative is not the centrally planned economy, but producer–consumer co-operatives and decentralized autonomous economic units. There should be a coalition between churches and trade unions throughout the world.[9] The moral bankruptcy of capitalism means that a *status confessionis* should be declared to resist capitalism in favour of common ownership.

Behind this thinking lie the views of Ulrich Duchrow, a West German theologian who writes much on economic affairs and who, like the Christendom Group, is prone to take over economic analyses (often of a neo-Marxist character) which suit his thesis, without understanding the subject.[10] In this context it is a theological point that is in question, the *status confessionis*. What is that? It is a phrase taken from the Formula of Concord (1573) to differentiate doctrines vital to the Christian faith and the very being of the church from things which are indifferent, like the vestments of officiating ministers. It was not used in a political context until Dietrich Bonhoeffer raised it after the Nazi accession to power in

Germany in 1933, which began the persecution of the Jews. Even so, he did not carry the agreement of the Confessing Church, the element of the Lutheran church which opposed Hitler; and the Barmen Declaration of 1934, which expressed its basic theological stand, did not refer to any specific public issue, but to the internal life of the church.

Duchrow wants to extend the *status confessionis* to political and economic issues, as against those Lutherans who say that these realms are wholly autonomous and a matter of indifference to the Christian. This is a spurious kind of apoliticism, which Duchrow is right to reject. However, the problem is not that such a declaration would split the church (as it would), but that there are few issues which are so black and white that it could be used on them, Duchrow holds that the 'Western' economic system is totally perverted and a gigantic conspiracy, threatening the continuation of human life and dignity. So to him it is a black-and-white issue. We have had reason to see how naive and over-simple this is. Duchrow also wants the concept to be extended to all weapons of mass destruction, and to the domination of nature by humans, both of which are more ambiguous issues than he allows.

The issue where a *status confessionis* has been declared is apartheid, by the Lutheran World Federation in 1977 and the World Alliance of Reformed Churches in 1982. But would it work as a critique of false ideologies, like possessive individualism? I myself would hold that Christians who support the wider use of the *status confessionis* seriously misunderstand the Christian faith, and that it only works if the ideology is totally false and the practice also corresponds with the ideology. In the case of apartheid this appears to be the case. For other issues it appears to be much too blunt an instrument to be helpful in dealing with the ambiguities of life.[11]

4. Donald Hay and Douglas Meeks

Since the relation of theological insights to the area of life which concerns economics is of permanent interest, it is not surprising that there is much ephemeral writing on the subject. From time to time, however, a book of considerable importance appears. In such cases it is rare to find an author equally at home in both disciplines, such are the demands of specialisms. Two recent major contributions concern us. The first is by Donald A. Hay, who is a lecturer in economics at Oxford University, and also a Reader (or lay officiant and preacher) in the Church of England; the second is by M. Douglas Meeks, who is professor of theology in an American seminary.[12]

Hay's book, which is that of an evangelical Christian who wishes to base his position in detail on the Bible, raises questions about how to use the Bible which are better considered in the next chapter. Meeks has much the same attitude with respect to doctrine, so that, too, can be considered there. Meanwhile, something needs to be said about their treatment of economic issues: more about Meeks than Hay, because Hay is a professional economist who knows what he is writing about, whereas Meeks is an interesting example of a theologian seriously trying to negotiate unfamiliar territory.

Hay does not distinguish economics from political economy and welfare economics as clearly as one would wish, nor does he give serious attention to how far there can be a search for common moral assumptions which can underpin the economic order in a plural world. But a study of his later chapters would remove many misunderstandings about the modern economic order which have been mentioned in this book. Democratic socialism does better than *laisser-faire* capitalism in his critique, and here he differs from his fellow evangelical Brian Griffiths. However, he warns against the danger of overmuch government planning on the grounds that attempts in this way to control the future are to substitute human agency for divine providence.

This is a good example of an illegitimate move from a basic doctrinal affirmation to one about how humans should cope with the changing features of the empirical world. It is one thing to think realistically about the hazards of forecasting and planning, and quite another to suspect it as an example of human pride. The theme of divine providence is a deep one, and mysterious, but it must surely be thought of in association with human endeavours and not put in opposition to them. Many things in the past which were thought of as acts of God, incapable of being influenced by humans, are now to varying degress within human control, and it is very likely that more will be. This does not diminish God. It is God's gift. However, it is safe to say that nothing will eliminate hazards in life which remain beyond human control, and a doctrine of divine providence cannot be dispensed with. Still, this is not the occasion to pursue the matter further.

For the rest, Hay writes well on the issue between 'Keynesians' (markets work well but they need help) and monetarists (markets work well if uncontrolled and unhindered) and, significantly in view of the tenor of the book, admits that the Bible has nothing directly to say on the matter; nor has it on the question of the use of exhaustible resources. Hay thinks they are to be used cautiously.

Meeks's book requires a fuller discussion. In one way it is an impressive attempt to deal with the economic realm, and has extensive references and footnotes, many of which are perceptive. It is therefore regrettable to have to mention confusions which arise from a basic uncertainty about economics. In the Foreword Meeks says that he does not want to take away the relative autonomy of the science of economics, but then says later that he regrets that God has been removed from the market. He adds that much modern economic theory assumes that the greedy character of human beings cannot be changed, and adds that scarcity is a false economic assumption. Both these comments show that he does not understand what economics is about, for the omission of the word *relative* before scarcity indicates a basic confusion which is fatal to much of the book.[13]

Meeks says that the Holy Spirit provides economic resources enough, thus calling scarcity into question (p. 171); this is a doctrinal argument similar to that by which Josiah Tucker tried to refute the mercantilists in the eighteenth century.[14] Later (p. 94), Meeks says that scarcity as a starting point will always produce an *oikos* (household) in which some are excluded from the means of life, when in pure theory (which is his starting point) this can only arise in the short term as workers change jobs. Another misconception is his remark (p. 132) that labour in a market economy always means unemployment for some, and the comment that self-interest as a motive for work involves an unprecedented demoralization is no better: we have unpacked the term self interest in economics in Chapter 3.

These misunderstandings do not prevent Meeks from making valid criticisms of the wider philosophy of the market. When the church has never taken economic power as seriously as it has political power, it is good to be reminded in the Introduction that political economy is concerned with the social relations of power in connection with gaining a livelihood; that the liberal tradition (*sic*, of the New Right!) denigrates politics by assuming that removing state power removes domination; that if the market is treated as the sole philosophy of relationship labour is treated impersonally; that a *political* economy is needed to illuminate the domination and a theology to deal with it (pp. 53–78); and that there is no such thing as a radically isolated individual.

However, Meeks falters in saying that modern economics must be challenged by theology because it squeezes out the biblical view of life, so that stewardship is ruled out (pp. 37ff). Rather, it is the case that a doctrine of stewardship *did* appear in Protestantism, as Wesley's Sermon on Money showed,[15] but it was made to bear all the weight of a social theology, and was too individualistic in its frame of reference. Meeks says he is not against the market but against its sole role in social life. This is a point of view which I share. But one has to be sure that one understands the market and the economic trends of one's own times if the precise role of the market and the framework needed around it are to be thought out. Meeks's criticism of the philosophy of market relations is mixed up with a criticism of economics based on a misunderstanding.

Meeks's positive suggestions are few. Nature must be given its rights and there must be justice for the land. (The confusions here are beyond our present concern.) There must be democratic control of investment and production, and democratic account-ability over the exercise of property rights. Companies laying off workers must provide their share of the cost of producing new jobs; and congregations must find diakonic work for those made redundant. (This is a sectarian position which leaves aside the role of the 'great society' as represented by the state, in dealing with a fundamental issue like unemployment.) Top managers must ulitmately be removable by the workers. Lastly, fundamental changes are needed in the rules of production and ownership with respect to decisions on capitalization.

Clearly all this is inconsequential where it is not vague. Behind it there is an alleged trinitarian basis which will be discussed in the next chapter.

A word needs to be added about Meeks's conception of God as an economist. It has no clear reference to the theological status of economics as a discipline with a certain autonomy which must be respected, but which has to be put in a wider reference, since it cannot settle issues of policy by itself. As we have noted, in so far as economics has escaped from the subjectivity of the realm of values (apart from efficiency in an economic sense) into the 'certainties' of science it has done so at the price of abstraction, and this has to be understood.[16] R.H. Tawney once called the state 'a serviceable drudge'. One could well say the same of economics. Meeks is playing with the concept of God as an economist rather than providing illumination. The word economics derives from the Greek *oikos*, which means a household. In the New Testament the term household is applied (among other terms) to the church; by extension it can cover the idea of the inhabited world as a household, regarded as the object of God's care. This raises the question as to what Meeks's theology has to say about the world apart from the Christian household, especially in view of his trinitarian stress. In his conclusion, the need for a community of common values is mentioned for the first time, but even then he moves on immediately to the church as a resurrection household. On what basis can Christians contribute to such a community of values? It will involve sustained dialogue with adherents of other religious faiths and with those of various humanist faiths. Some will urge that humans must stand together because of their common rationality; others that they must stand together because of their common humanity,[17] and this can be spelled out in terms of different human characteristics, such as conscience. It is all very relevant to the theme of God the economist as interpreted by Meeks, but he does not embark on it.

5. Roman Catholic teaching

I turn to recent Roman Catholic teaching.[18] The official documents from the papacy tend to stress the continuity in the church's social teaching, even though, as we have seen, parts of it fade away, as did that on usury, or are radically changed, as those on slavery and religious freedom.[19] Recently, except in the matter of sexual ethics, a more historical approach has been followed, instead of a more static deduction from immutable first principles. There has been a shift to concern for the person, personal freedom and equality, and personal decision-making, rather than a stress on obedience, inequality and order. The Pastoral Constitution of the Second Vatican Council, *Gaudium et Spes* (1965), was much more historical than previous documents, and the papal letter *Octogesima Adveniens* (1971) was even more so. These are tendencies, not absolute distinctions, for John Paul II seems a little wary of too historical an approach, as leading to an unacceptable relativism and a threat to a unified point of view emanating from the Vatican. His own emphasis on the personal in *Laborem Exercens* (1981) is more of a philosophical reflection, against an existential background. Nevertheless, the general tone of official teaching is some way from the traditional sharp distinction between the teaching church and the learning church, and the call to the faithful laity to follow their appointed pastors like 'docile sheep'. Similarly, the Vatican was cautious about talk of human rights, so that *Pacem in Terris* (1963) is the first major treatment of them.

Laborem Exercens (1981) stresses work as fundamental (manual work seems to be in mind and there may be a touch of archaism here), and very significantly states that man is not just one among other factors of production, as in liberal capitalism; rather, human beings have priority over things. The right to private property in church teaching is subordinated to the right of common use, and adaptations to the rights of ownership in the means of production are needed. Moreover, the state must act positively against unemployment by concrete planning. The encyclical is somewhat impressionistic. There is no discussion of management. It appears to favour workers' co-operatives, but this may be only an appearance. There is no precise analysis of the market, which is associated with 'materialism'. There is too easy a separation, when talking of trade unions, between industry and politics (even more difficult if the state is the employer), which allows the church to avoid the charge of being political.[20]

Sollicitudo Rei Socialis (1988) includes new elements within its reference to continuity and renewal in church social teaching. These are: 1. a preferential option for the poor (which shows the influence of Latin American liberation theology);[21] 2. a reference to structural as distinct from personal sin (perhaps reflecting the same influence), but it rather backs away from this; 3. ecological issues, briefly listed. The dignity of the person again underlies it, much more than human sin. The analysis of the economic order is perfunctory. There is a reference to the consuming desire for profit and the thirst for power, but there is no precise analysis of the economic order, especially with respect to the role of profits. The responsibility of all for all is finely stated (far from possessive individualism), but how to handle the perennial conflicts of interest in the economic and political order within this responsibility is not faced. Churches find it hard to deal with structural sin because they themselves are involved in the structures which cause it. It is easier to remain at the level of exhorting individuals and, moreover, addressing nations as if they are individuals, as John Paul does here.

As far as economics is concerned, the Pope says that he is offering principles of reflection, criteria of judgments and directions for action, and that this church teaching draws on the Bible, rational reflection and the human sciences. It is tacitly assumed that the human sciences will agree with church teaching. But what if they do not? Economics is a human science. The fact that it has a certain autonomy is important, but its parameters and the relation of economic efficiency to other values needs exploration. This question is more subtle than the sharp separation implied, which indeed is more like that found in much traditional Lutheranism.[22]

The other recent source of (unofficial) Roman Catholic teaching is that of the bishops of the USA.[23] The bishops' conference had intended to write a pastoral letter on capitalism, but changed its focus and omitted an analysis of it, concentrating on wealth distribution, not its creation. The authority they claim for their work is modestly at the level of prudence. The method they adopted was that suggested by *Octogesima Adveniens* (1971), and is a great improvement on the secretive way papal teaching is produced. Apart from hearing a wide variety of witnesses, prior drafts were issued for comment before the text was finalized. Its basis is biblical, summed up in the phrase 'the dignity of the human person in community with others', akin to St Paul's understanding of *koinonia* (community or fellowship) applied to the church. The Bible is supplemented by reference to the common good (*Gaudium et Spes* 36), and the concept of subsidiarity (*Quadragesimo Anno* 79).

The letter is critical of the economic inequalities in the USA (1 in 7 being poor by the government's own standards, and 50% of the financial assets being held by 2% of the population). A rate of 7–8% unemployment is unacceptable. Critics of the letter from the left said that its idealism ignored fundamental social conflicts. Critics from the right were far more common, and they were along the lines of the New Right: distrust of government 'interference', denial of social justice as an intelligible concept, a stress on the importance of the creation of wealth, and the demand that the church should stick to ends and not get involved with means.

This outlook was expressed by the twenty-seven chief executives of major business corporations who upstaged the bishops' letter by issuing their lay report on the previous day. It draws on the same Roman Catholic teaching to show that the freedom of the individual is crucial. Private ownership keeps power dispersed, encourages wide stewardship and promotes the creation of wealth. Scepticism of government activity is expressed because of its inefficiencies and liability to abuse of power; the skills and risks involved in creating wealth are stressed; voluntary action by lay folk should set out to prevent a culture of dependency.

So this chapter ends where it began, with by far the most powerful among the rare articulate Christian endorsements of the ideology of the New Right.

The theological bases of these Christian comments needs further exploration. This is particularly the case with respect to the Bible. It is stressed not only by evangelical Christians but also by Roman Catholics. We have just seen that the USA bishops' letter is based on the Bible (in fact on the concepts of creation), covenant and community drawn from scripture). It is to these issues that we turn in the next chapter.

7 The Bible, Doctrine and Economic Issues

Putting things as simply as possible, we can say that decision-making in the Christian life means both acting from the right motive and making the right decision in particular cases. It means having a sensitive conscience which uses its power of reasoning on moral issues with discernment. Motivation involves what the catholic tradition calls 'spiritual formation', including the practice of public worship and private prayer, which themselves embrace reflection on Christian sources in the Bible and the tradition of doctrine. It also involves a mutual building up within the Christian community of perceptiveness by discussion, dialogue and, on occasions, pastoral counselling. All this is not the direct concern of this book. Bringing these resources to bear on particular issues is our concern. How this is done applies, of course, to every area of life, personal and social, but we are focussing on economic issues.

It is evident that some knowledge of the data of these issues is indispensable, even if it is often not as adequate as we would like. If we do not know the data we cannot focus on the issue. It is also evident that the data cannot come from the Bible or doctrine. They can only come from understanding evidence in the present. That is why in respect of many of the issues an element of expertise is needed on which to draw (though not uncritically). But expertise by itself does not settle the matter. The further question is how we relate the two elements needed in ethical decision-making: the Bible and the doctrinal tradition on the one hand, and the data of the contemporary world on the other. How much detail can we derive from them? Certainly the former give us an understanding of human life and destiny (or, put another way, of nature, humanity and God), which then has to be brought alongside our analysis of 'what is going on' in our contemporary situation.

I suggest that there is a reciprocal relation between the two. The Christian sources give us criteria which are important in selecting and interpreting from the mass of contemporary data. These criteria are not necessarily peculiar to Christianity, but may overlap at times with those of other faiths, religious and humanist. But the data may also reflect back on our understanding of the Christian sources and lead us to reflect on them anew, instead of inheriting them as a fixed and unchangeable deposit from the past. For example, the human sciences of psychology and sociology have modified and enriched the understanding of the personal which is central to Christian faith. In this way an ongoing reflection on our past in the light of our experience of the present is always at work in the church at every level, from church leaders and governing bodies downwards to particular congregations, and to groups thinking and praying together within congregations, or groups of Christians with similar vocational concerns meeting together in medicine, education, industry and commerce, administration or the arts.

I am broadly content with this account. Of course, it can be greatly expanded, and would need to be in a thorough exposition of method in Christian ethics. Many, however, are unhappy with it. To them it seems altogether too contextual and relativistic. It seems to be in danger of selling out to whatever notions are popular with the intelligentsia (or, less likely, the 'workers') at a given moment. It reminds them of Dean Inge's remark that he who marries the spirit of the age soon finds himself a widower in the next. They want something much more fixed and detailed. This is particularly the case with the Bible.

1. The use of the Bible

Behind this search for more detailed and unchangeable material from the Bible lies a belief, particularly in some evangelical circles, that God is the author of scripture, and that every text therefore has potential permanent authority. It is assumed that God reveals himself to humans through the words of scripture without any of the cultural and relativizing factors and shifts in the meanings of words which occur when humans communicate by words with one another. This attitude is reinforced by the current practice of saying 'This is the word of the Lord' after reading in church services a non-gospel passage from the Bible. Thus an epistle from St Paul to one of the churches is turned into an epistle from God to St Paul. By contrast there is much to be said for the traditional Anglican appeal to scripture, tradition and reason.[1] Indeed the Bible alone has not proved enough to establish doctrine. The church had in fact to go outside it in order to protect its understanding of Christ at the time of the Arian controversy, and its wording is embodied in the 'Nicene' Creed. Tradition alone also will not do,[2] or the church would never do anything for the first time.[3] Reason is important: not the deductive reason which can draw logical conclusions from a premiss, but a historical and critical reason.[4] However, reason must also have the Bible and tradition to work on, or it will be conjuring up rational abstractions, because the Christian faith is rooted in the life and ministry of Jesus, which occurred at a particular time and place in history.

The kingdom of God is the focus of Jesus' ministry: a radical understanding of God's way of exercising his rule as king or sovereign over his creation, and one which is always seeking expression in human life and institutions and always transcending any particular expression. Jesus did not give us detailed moral rules, even on marriage and divorce,[5] or on what precisely is due to the state (Caesar). His teaching is questioning, illuminating, liberating, imaginative and life-giving. There are indeed many contextual decisions elsewhere in the Bible, but we cannot move directly from them to the modern world. In the New Testament they are concerned with how the people of God should behave to one another (for instance, Paul says they should not go to law against one another in secular courts),[6] and how they should relate to the state. In the Old Testament this was not a problem because church and state were one kingdom: Israel was a theocracy. From New Testament times there has always been a problem because there are two kingdoms, both God's kingdoms, but with different tasks. The Christendom situation in Europe (pre-supposed by Hooker in England) which united them again is now almost gone; it was an exception in Christian history, in the course of which the church has lived under a great variety of state authorities.

The National Evangelical Anglican conference at Nottingham in 1977 said very wisely that: 1. the words of scripture are to be understood in their context; 2. the context is to be understood in terms of the cultural assumptions of the writers; 3. there is need for alertness to our own cultural assumptions.[7] However, many evangelicals, and others, have not accepted this, or do not follow it in practice.[8]

Sometimes the attempt is made to take a single text or a catena of texts as a simple rule or example. Hundreds of Puritan sermons were preached in the year after the execution of Charles I, 1648–49, on the text of Psalm 149.8, which has the words: 'To bind their kings in chains; and their nobles with links of iron.' Karl Barth, in a startling passage in 'The Christian Community and the Civil Community', says that because Jesus is the light of the world there must be no secret diplomacy.[9] In the nineteenth century a strong *defence* of slavery was advanced by detailing biblical texts, and in this century homosexuality is *attacked* by the same method.[10] Many other examples could be quoted.

However, some who see the inadequacy of quoting texts in this way want to derive from them *principles* which can then be followed in a contemporary context. How well does this work? I take three examples.

1. A paper from the Cambridge (UK) Jubilee Centre[11] says that we should establish the intention of the original text in its social context (for this is God himself speaking), then look for analogies or situational correspondences between the situation today and that in the Bible, and then apply the moral principle involved. If the Old Testament says in Leviticus 25 that all land is to be returned to the original owners every fifty years, we can work back by abstraction to the need for justice in economic life. We are to exclude in the Old Testament requirements which (*a*) are part of the sacrificial law; (*b*) are designed to make Israel exclusive of others; (*c*) assert that Israel is executing God's judgment on Canaan; (*d*) are purely theocratic, since church and state were one Kingdom. In the New Testament we are to exclude: (*a*) a command addressed to an individual; (*b*) one addressed to the church as an economic community. The Old Testament is to be a paradigm for a pattern of relationships between key institutions – family, kinship, state, land, capital and community – which is to be replicated today 'in certain fundamental respects'. In practice, this leads to a strong emphasis in Jubilee Centre publications on the extended family as against the state. But in so far as content can be given to it, the requirement that such a paradigmatic correspondence between Israel's institutions in biblical

times and the ones today, whether we live in the First, Second or Third Worlds, seems an arbitrary restriction.

2. Associated with the same group is a campaign for keeping Sunday special, in the sense of restrictions on trading activities so that it remains different from the other six days of the week. The four principles underlying the campaign are all alleged to be biblically based, but whatever we may think of them, the texts quoted will not work as a basis for the principles. (*a*) The purpose behind the sabbath is love to God, so that we do not give him the odd bits of our time but the best. The text here is Luke 10.27, which is Jesus' two-fold summary of the Torah as love of God and neighbour. (*b*) The sabbath protects the low-income worker from pressure to work seven days a week. The text is Deuteronomy 5.12–16 (a variation of Exodus 20), where the weight falls on the deliverance from Egypt, though the welfare of slaves is mentioned. (*c*) Family, community and church life are preserved if everyone is at leisure at the same time. Here the Exodus 10.8–11 passage is quoted, but that stresses that the family should keep the sabbath not because of the family, but because God keeps it. (*d*) The sabbath follows a regular rhythm of work and rest which is God's design. The quotation is Genesis 2.3, but this is not concerned with biological rhythms but with God the creator.

It seems clear that in the Old Testament, in a one-kingdom situation, the sabbath is a stretch of time to be set apart for God. In the New Testament it also seems clear that there is no stress on keeping any day special in the sense intended by the four principles. These may very well be wise principles, but they cannot be sustained by quoting texts in the way proposed. That Christians should specially worship together on Sunday, a new day celebrating Jesus' triumph over death, is quite another matter. That work and leisure are both divine gifts is also another matter. What state regulation should be, and how workers should be safeguarded against unjust demands by employers in a competitive society, is yet a third question.

3. An extended attempt to arrive at biblical principles for the economic order is made by Donald Hay in the book referred to in Chapter 6.[12] He derives eight principles by what he calls a process of deduction and imaginative reflection from the great biblical themes of creation, fall, judgment and the people of God. They are to be applicable to all people, not just to the people

of God, and to be timeless and consistent. They are in three groups.

The first group is concerned with creation and human dominion. (*a*) Man must use the resources of creation to provide for his existence, but he must not waste or destroy the created order (the texts quoted are given in n. 12 below). (*b*) Every person has a calling to exercise stewardship of resources and talents. (*c*) Stewardship implies responsibility to determine the disposition of resources. Each person is accountable to God for his stewardship.

The second group is concerned with man and his work. (*d*) Man has a right and obligation to work. (*e*) Work is the means of exercising stewardship. In his work man should have access to resources and control over them. (*f*) Work is a social activity in which men co-operate as stewards of their individual talents, and as joint stewards of resources.

The last section concerns the distribution of goods. (*g*) Every person has a right to share in God's provision for mankind for their basic needs of food, clothing and shelter. These needs are primarily to be met by productive work. (*h*) Personal stewardship of these resources does not imply the right to consume the entire produce of the resources. The rich have an obligation to help the poor who cannot provide for themselves by work.

In the last four chapters of his book Hay does not make much direct use of these biblical principles, which he has rather laboriously erected on a selection of texts. This is perhaps less surprising when one considers the very different milieu out of which the texts come, not least the relative scarcity of the pre-industrial world as compared with the relative abundance for one-third of the world's population today. Hay calls for a simple life-style in the rich countries (and we shall have to consider this in connection with economic growth in the next chapter). He issues a general doctrinal, rather than directly biblical, warning against trying to control the future too much instead of relying on divine providence, a sentiment which needs very careful unpacking if a dubious meaning is not to be given to it. Hay says that the extinction of a species is against biblical principles, but it is not obvious why God will allow 'nature' to bring this about in the course of evolution whilst humans must not.

In short, in these four chapters, which contain a great deal of valuable analysis of different economic systems and the current national and international economic situation, there are occasional references to the Bible, but nothing like the closeness which the careful working-out of the eight principles would lead one to expect. I myself once wove the various references to the state in the New Testament into a principle. As far as I could see, they amount to saying that when the state is favourable to the church it should be unqualifiedly supported, and when it is hostile it should be unqualifiedly opposed. This is obviously useless as a principle to guide Christians in the many different situations of church and state in the modern world, and is not even adequate if a state's attitude is clearly for or against church institutions. Far better to use these texts as building-blocks out of which to construct a theology of the state and of church and state relations, amplifying it in accordance with ongoing experience.

It is important to realize what the Bible presupposes, but does not explicitly justify. Above all it presupposes the reality of God. Then, within its drama of creation, fall, the people of God (elected and then recreated in Christ) and the last things, it presupposes the creation ordinances of family, work, political (state) authority and culture. It does not set out to be a textbook of sociological or political theory. Its very varied forms of literature, particularly its narratives and parables, stir the imagination and inform the judgment by deepening our powers of discernment. But its many particular moral commands and ethical judgments must always be set in their context. Few would dispute this in some cases, like the judgment (which seems incautious even at the time) in Titus 1.12 of the Cretans that 'it was a Cretan prophet, one of their own countrymen, who said "Cretans were ever liars, vicious brutes, lazy gluttons" – and how truly he spoke!'

However, the thirty-six imperatives in I Corinthians 7, especially the six questions about marriage that St Paul answers, have often not been considered in relation to his expectation of the imminent *parousia* (v. 29). In the light of this, Paul's judgment that in the last analysis marriage is a distraction from the single-minded service of God has some force; apart from this expectation it has had a most unfortunate effect on Christian thought in subsequent centuries. Or, to take one more illustration, Paul's advice to Christians (in I Cor. 8) in connection with eating food offered to idols (that is to say, food which had previously been part of a ceremony in a temple), that those who see no harm in it should give way to those who have scruples, because it is after all a minor matter, may well

have been wise in that particular situation. However, if it is turned
into a general principle, it leads to a highly restrictive form of
Christian living aimed at not offending those Christians who see
harm in such things as card-playing, dancing and games on Sunday
– to say nothing of alcoholic drinks. The fact is that the ethical
material in the Bible is rich and diverse. Selections from its texts
can be made to support varied attitudes, and attempts to weave
them into a unified pattern which can then be applied to the
modern world are not convincing.[13]

The witness to Jesus is the focus of the Bible. Christians read the
Old Testament to see how he fulfilled (and negated) it; and the rest
of the New Testament apart from the Gospels is the story of the
new community he inaugurated to be a herald of the kingdom of God
as he taught and lived it. It is the more significant that the Gospels
contain no detailed rules for individual or social life (not even on
marriage, as I have mentioned), either in the church fellowship or
for the state. They have to be worked at down the centuries, as St
Paul worked at them in the earliest decades of the church. That is
what makes a study of his efforts so important, even though he lived
in a much less complex and differentiated society than that of today.

These particular efforts take place within the cosmic drama
which the classical Christian doctrines derive from the Bible:
creation, fall, incarnation, atonement, the church, and the last
things. These link nature, humans and God in one vision. Attempts
are made to jump directly from them to too detailed conclusions, as
we shall see in the next section. Moreover they themselves have
been interpreted in different ways in accordance with the reciprocal
relation between the data of the Christian tradition and the
changing cultural situation, to which I have also already referred –
particularly depending on whether it is thought of as static or
dynamic. Nevertheless, certain insights of fundamental importance
can be drawn from Christian doctrine, though we can do more than
indicate them here. Among them is the significance of humans as
made in God's image: finite but free to be creative, yet 'fallen'; then
re-created through Jesus, renewed, and given a hope which is both
terrestrial and celestial. A terrestrial hope, because the creation
is good and humans are able to work with it if they use their powers
as God intends; a celestial hope, because what God has in store
transcends the world of time and space and cannot be completed in
the short time-span of humanity.

There is also a universalism here which transcends differences of sex and colour: it is specially concerned for the 'poor' (not only those who are economically poor but all society's rejects, as the ministry of Jesus shows); it is concerned for what makes for community, so that people feel at ease with one another; it is aware of human frailties and sins and so is alert to the abuse of power, but also to the need to use it to arrive at a tolerable resolution of the conflicts of interest which arise in human history between individuals and groups;[14] and because of this it does not give unqualified support to the necessary but inevitably transient settlements of such conflicts as humans from time to time arrive at. This last is not because Christians are pessimists, but because they are aware of the ambiguities of life, yet still have a vision which inspires them to venture further in response to the call and challenge of the kingdom of God.[15]

The upshot is that the Bible is to be taken seriously but not woodenly. It is for the regular nourishment of the spirit (like holy communion), and is not a source of detailed rules of conduct.

2. The use of doctrine

Those theologians who move from theology to the social order often show two tendencies which are not helpful: they isolate and exaggerate the direct effect of some doctrine on the social and political order, ignoring the social factors influencing the context in which it is interpreted; or they draw detailed contents from doctrine as others do from a biblical text. This is not to deny that theological doctrines can operate as independent variables in human society. There is no reason to suppose that economic and cultural factors alone are independent variables. Rather, as I have already stressed, theological and cultural factors act reciprocally upon one another. Theologians need to remember this. Some, for instance, have argued that a stress on divine grace leads to a relaxation of ethical endeavour. Yet set in the dynamic context of the development of capitalism it had the reverse effect, as Weber's thesis on the relation of Calvinism to capitalism showed. Or again, monotheism has been said by Moltmann to favour totalitarianism, or by Meeks individualism, both very implausibly. These charges occur in connection with discussions of the importance of the doctrine of the Trinity for a social theology. It is worth considering it.

The doctrine of the Trinity became central to the Christian faith for a simple but basic reason. The first Christians, who were all Jews, found themselves worshipping God through Jesus Christ. The most common end today to public prayers to God is still 'through Jesus Christ our Lord'. Jews above all others were profound believers in *one* God. They alone succeeded in excluding themselves from worshipping the gods of the state religion of the Roman Empire. So how could believers in one God worship him through Jesus Christ? Christianity seemed, and still seems to monotheistic Jews and Muslims, to be idolatrous. The New Testament offered fragmentary and not always consistent evidence, and it took the church four hundred years, often of very rocky controversy, to arrive at an expression of its faith in the words of the doctrine of the Trinity. It was seen that the worship of God through Jesus required some indication in words of what must be a self-differentiation in God; his outreach to us suggests this. But how to express it?

The words at hand came from the contemporary Greek and Latin vocabulary. The word 'person' which was used to express the doctrine of the Trinity (three persons but one God) had the sense of a mask or, in a more self-involved way, of a role on stage or, still more, in society. (We occasionally use the term when a list of the cast in a play is headed *dramatis personae*, though this is dying out.) This is far from the concept of person which is developed in a rich way in the modern sense of the term personality. Classical Christianity did not go that way, for it was afraid of straying into a belief in three gods, and being back in polytheism, a danger from which Judaism had emancipated the Judaeo-Christian tradition. Different strains in trinitarian teaching have always existed.[16] Classical orthodoxy elaborated the doctrine of *perichoresis*, according to which each 'person' of the Trinity, Father, Son and Spirit, interpenetrates the other in a kind of mystical unity. Clearly words are strained to the limit when used as in this doctrine to speak of the innermost nature of God.

Recently there has been a revival of a 'social' doctrine of the Trinity, stressing a quasi-social unit of what gets near to being thought of as a society of three personal beings (rather like mediaeval art, which sometimes portrayed the Trinity as three human figures).[17] Leonardo Boff, a Latin American liberation theologian, has the same stress. He sees the human experience of community as the most appropriate *analogy* for giving us a glimpse into the nature of the triune God in which three divine persons relate to each other, and as the basis for us to create communities of love.[18] What has happened? We search for an analogy from human life to apply to God and then derive back from it a pattern for society, as if a new source of illumination had been discerned.

Meeks, in the book we considered in Chapter 6, writes in a similar fashion. If he talks of God the economist, he also talks of the economy of God, as a triune community of persons. The work of the Trinity is distinctive, co-operative and egalitarian (*perichoresis*); it is the work of self-giving love.[19] Therefore human work must not be coercively integrated. Meeks accompanies this with a polemic against a more unitary view of God as the inspirer of market forces. This, he argues, justifies structures of domination, and humans have taken over this view in a secularized form in the market system.[20] The doctrine of the consumer as king in the market reflects the idea of the authoritarian monotheistic God. This is a highly implausible theological basis on which to criticize the idea of the market, which in so far as it derives by several removes from Christian theology is much more related to the concept of personal responsibility. The market's excessive individualism, and forgetfulness that persons are what they are in the communities which form them and relate them to each other, is much better criticized from a key New Testament concept like *koinonia*, which we translate as fellowship or communion. We shall return to this.

Another doctrine from which too detailed deductions have been made is natural law. It is a confusing term, ambiguous even when it was considered self-evident. It is the source of a vast literature.[21] It does not, properly understood, refer to a law of physical nature, as the laws of natural science are often thought of, nor a law enacted by a state or local authority, but to a moral law which human beings know they are bound by, not because it has been imposed on them by an outside authority, but because they themselves recognize its authority. Natural law is self-imposed, but responds to what is understood as a moral fact of life. One does not have to be 'religious', still less a Christian, to recognize it, though Christians believe that it is a moral order inherent in God's universe, one which has led to the appearance of persons in it. Persons can recognize it because of their conscience, or power of reflection on moral (ethical) matters. But what is the *content* of natural law? The basic formulation of it is that 'the good is to be done and the evil avoided'. That is to say that what conscience approves should be followed, and what it does not approve should be shunned. To recognize this is a characteristic of *human* beings. Those who do not follow the natural law know that they are doing wrong.

Many complications follow from this vital truth about humanity. What is thought to be good and evil, or right and wrong, in particular cases varies greatly. How does one avoid prejudice in one's judgments? All the complications, however, are capable of resolution, as far as inevitable uncertainties in ethical judgments allow. The trouble has been that there has been a tendency to derive detail from the doctrine of natural law, and then the customs of one's own time tend to be thought of as natural, and deviations from them as unnatural.

St Paul gives us an example of this first error in his reference to the length of men's and women's hair (I Cor. 11.14f.). And we have already seen how Aristotle said that, physically, money could not breed, and therefore it was unnatural to charge interest for the use of it. Artificial insemination of animals (let alone humans) has been held to be unnatural. So has the use of chemicals in farming as against organic farming. If one argues in this way, there is no need to consider the ethical arguments for and against in such issues; one rules out a practice on *a priori* grounds as being 'unnatural' – that is to say contrary to natural law. These examples shade into an attempt to move directly from a basic physical fact of life to a detailed ethical conclusion and not from its personal context in human relations.

A controversy continues in Roman Catholic moral theology in this area. Thus the organs of speech exist to speak what is true. Therefore lying is unnatural. But what is to count as lying? An unbelievably complex debate developed over centuries in order to allow for exceptions to the morally absurd situations which occur if the prohibition is taken as a fixed rule. In a relational context it becomes a question of who has a right to the truth, and to what extent? Similarly, an inspection of the genital organs is said to show us that they are meant for procreation. Therefore any use of them in sexual intercourse which tries to prevent such an outcome is 'unnatural'. This is one of the arguments in the papal encyclical *Humanae Vitae* (1968) condemning contraception. The oddity of such arguments is that in theory what is 'natural' and 'unnatural' should be clear to all men and women of good will. In fact the arguments do not carry conviction to vast numbers of people, and the church has to bring in the weight of its authority to reinforce them and to stem, largely in vain, a plurality of opinion within its own borders. Such a use of natural law is no basis for detailed conclusions on economic or any other issues.

Understanding natural law as saying that the realm of the moral is natural to humans is another matter. But we do not know what humans have it in them to be, though we can be sure that they will remain finite, free and fallen. Sin in its subtlest forms will feed on virtues and achievements, and is likely to corrupt them. So an earthly utopian economic order is ruled out. There will always be trade-offs, considerations to be balanced against one another. But that is no reason for pessimism, because we do not live within fixed structures, whether in nature or human society, which cannot be improved: quite the contrary.

3. From the Bible and doctrine to contemporary issues

Bringing Christian insights to bear on the ongoing issues in the modern world, not least in the economic order, is not easy. Given the radical Christian understanding of the kingdom or rule of God, it is not hard to denounce what is wrong. And there is always a place for the prophet who challenges complacency. But what is the next step?[22] Criticizing ideologies from such a perspective is important, because uncritical ideologists are terrible simplifiers. It is not hard to see that conservatism, liberalism and socialism each have their strengths and weaknesses from the point of view of a social theology. Moreover, those who criticize must apply their critique to themselves, whether churches or individuals, because the Christian faith does not come to us uninfluenced by the cultural constraints of history. Beyond that, more detailed work is needed to get further than generalities. This involves assessing facts and trends, and the likely consequences of available options. For this some expertise is needed. It is said that only an expert can test an expert. But we have seen that this is only half true. In the last resort we ourselves have to come to an opinion about experts.

Beyond the expert there is personal experience of, at any level, the issues on which decisions have to be made.[23] Particular attention needs to be paid to, and to draw in, that of those marginalized in society, who frequently fail to get a hearing. Opinion is best formed by illuminating a middle ground, between generalities which can be agreed because no application of them is mentioned, and detailed policy recommendations, where the selection and weighing of evidence and estimates of the consequences of specific policies are likely to have so many uncertainties as to make general agreement unlikely. At a middle level agreement may be reached on the broad policy direction in which to move (and possibly on the ruling out of some options as undesirable), leaving those committed to the direction to find their different ways to implement it.[24] This is often how things happen in party politics. There is a certain level of consent beneath the differences, so that on gaining power one party does not set out to undo all that has gone before. But this does not always happen. If Christians cannot agree at a middle level, the remaining possibility is to identify the different positions and then ask advocates of each to formulate the questions they want to ask advocates of the others, and to ask each to listen to and address the questions the others put to them. In this way different decisions of integrity can still be made by Christians who acknowledge their common allegiance, beyond their differences, to their one Lord.

At the same time churches and individual Christians have a duty to search for as much common ground as possible with adherents of other faiths. God has put us in his creation cheek by jowl in a world of structures of work, politics and culture, not by virtue of our Christian faith but as human beings. We are bound up with others in the bundle of humanity not by our choice but by God's creative purpose. His will is for human flourishing for others in these structures as much as for us. We must seek out and work with whoever will work to further that flourishing, wherever they are to be found. It is dangerous always to be wanting to say or stand for something that is so distinctively Christian that no one else is likely to see the force of it.[25]

The organs of expressing Christian judgments are as varied as the church itself. It is best of all if they are made ecumenically. But they can be made by central, regional or local units (like one congregation or parish), by single-issue groups (like Church Action on Poverty), by working with other groups (like Age Concern), and by symbolic actions to awaken the indifferent from apathy.

All this illustrates the ambiguities in Christian faith and ethics. There are tensions in the world of doctrine and political economy between original sin and original righteousness, between grace and works, between seeing the kingdom of God as already here and experienced and concentrating on its final consummation, between economic efficiency and cushioning individuals and groups against the hardships of change, between freedom to hire labour or not and the right to work, between liberty and equality, and between freedom (in which your destiny is in your own hands) and constraint (through lack of necessities).

There is the further problem of risk assessment, mentioned in Chapter 2 (section 3). It involves identifying and evaluating risks before deciding on policies, and assessing them after the implementation of decisions. These problems can be summed up in the question, 'How do we live with change?' Safety first is not a wise policy in most cases, certainly not as a general principle.[26] Humans cannot be immune from change; but how far can they be expected constantly to adjust to it? Again, we must be ready for the unexpected, but what is truly unexpected cannot be the basis of present decisions. Vision is needed, so that we do not take the present too uncritically; but there must be a stability of conviction which undergirds the ambiguities of life. This book is written from the conviction that the Christian faith is a blessing before it is a task, and that it gives us the stability we need. (I fully accept that there are other souces of stability available in the world, and I am not concerned in this context to compare and contrast them.)

A most vexing area of economic decisions is that of the responsibilities of the relatively affluent countries of the 'North' to the relatively, and in many cases absolutely, poor countries of the 'South'. Here I move with some uncertainty. But in order to earth the reflections of this book in immediate concerns I turn in the last chapter to these international economic issues and to their domestic repercussions.

8 North–South: The Responsibilities of Affluence

1. A global economy

Technological changes and two world wars have produced a global economy. Since the Bretton Woods conference of 1944 which set up a system of relatively fixed exchange rates, there has been an enormous growth of world population, productivity and trade. Bretton Woods envisaged an International Trade Organization as well as the International Monetary Fund and the World Bank. However, its constitution was never ratified, and instead a modified version of it was founded in 1947, the General Agreement on Tariffs and Trade (GATT), which has nearly one hundred member states. It has operated by inducing countries reciprocally to lower tariff barriers; to operate a most-favoured nation arrangement whereby any concession by one nation to another applies all round; and to replace non-tariff barriers by tariffs, and then reduce these. As a result, tariff barriers have dropped from an average of 40% to 5%.

After twenty-five years the relatively fixed currency system broke up, and by 1973 the major currencies were floating. The quadrupling of oil prices in 1973–4 halted economic growth on the basis of cheap energy. Huge surpluses of liquid cash from the oil-producing countries were recycled, by banks and private operators, to the OECD and Third World countries, and since then there has been a vast quantity of international mobile finance. Given the current degree of world integration, it is no longer possible to have unco-ordinated national economic policies by which countries attempt to 'go it alone'. France tried in 1981–2 and failed. Keynes in his day could assume that the United Kingdom was sufficiently powerful to lead an expansionist trade policy. Today the USA is the only country which is conceivably capable of managing the world's trading system, but even it cannot have the predominant role it had in 1944. Co-ordination of national economic policies is extremely difficult because each country wants to operate on its own if it can; short-term and long-term interests often conflict, and the short-term ones nearly always win. Yet the constraint remains, that an economy cannot be run efficiently if there are violent changes in the exchange rate, and the reactions of all major countries govern that. It cannot be determined nationally. That is why the European Monetary System with its Exchange Rate Mechanism is of such importance.

However, all is not well with GATT. Indeed, some think it is dead. It has never been followed whole-heartedly, even though it modified its rules to allow for temporary emergencies, and for anti-dumping duties if, for instance, goods were exported at a lower price than in the home market. Moreover, Third World countries were allowed a differential status which allowed them to restrict imports. All these, incidentally, are examples of the eighteenth-century mercantilist thinking still influential in GATT. We shall return to this very shortly. Furthermore, ways have been found for getting round GATT by voluntary export restraints (as with Japanese cars in Britain) and quota arrangements. Protectionist forces are powerful.[1] There is talk of 'managed trade'; and we may find GATT replaced by three trading blocks based on USA and the Americas, Europe, and Japan and the Asian-Pacific region. The best that can be said of that is that it would at least be better than merely bilateral trade deals.

What do I mean by 'better'? I am thinking in terms of economic efficiency in the sense of maximizing what it is possible to do, other things being equal, with the relatively scarce resources at our disposal. As has been emphasized, there are other things which governments and electorates may wish to consider, but one wants to be sure that the economic costs of pursuing them are realized. Electorates find trade policies obscure and complicated. Governments know this and, subject as they are to all kinds of pressures from vested interests, some of them economically and politically powerful, are often tempted to fudge trade matters in a way which impoverishes the general good in favour of a partial interest.

Ignorance of these basic economic facts of life makes it easier for mercantilism, a form of economic nationalism, to flourish. The case for free trade is that it maximizes the productivity of relatively scarce resources. It leads each state to concentrate on what it can do most efficiently (in the economic sense). Since no state can do everything, and since none has unlimited resources, each, on free trade principles, should do what it is relatively best at, in which it has a comparative advantage or, putting it the other way, the smallest disadvantage. (Adam Smith pointed out that wine could be produced in Scotland if consumers were prepared to pay the cost of its enormous disadvantage.) Economically a state will benefit by free trade even if others do not reciprocate. This is *politically* a hard lesson to accept; there will be strong political pressures to retaliate in kind against the goods and services of another state which will not operate on a free-trade basis, even though the retaliator will be economically poorer as a result.

Of course, complete free trade is an 'ideal' construct which ignores all other human considerations, including political ones. It excludes problems of political power. Those states which have greater human and natural resources find that their economic power becomes political power. It has been one of the handicaps of the Third World countries that they have had a lack of bargaining power in international institutions such as the International Monetary Fund and the World Bank. They have been further disadvantaged because they have not always agreed among themselves. Partly the lack is an inevitable fact of life, snce natural resources (like personal endowments) are very unevenly distributed. How far Third World countries can be given more power is a question to consider later. However, in so far as GATT rules are followed, these countries are certainly given more economic power than by more restricted trade agreements. There are signs that this is being better appreciated by them, and that they are beginning to think there is more to be said for a broadly free-trade approach than they had thought. It is the wealthy Northern countries, the USA and the European Community, who are inclined to persist in and reinforce protectionist tendencies.

2. The need for economic growth in the Third World

The economies of the Third World are in fact growing, but at very different rates. In the decade 1980–1990 Africa grew at the rate of

1% p.a., Latin America at 1½%, South Asia at 5.5% and East Asia at 8.4%. Yet in many ways it was a lost decade. The absolute number of those living in poverty probably increased. Malnutrition is all the time quietly killing more than the periodic famines which attract attention, and a mood of pessimism has developed because of the failure of the United Nations' plans for a new economic order. And now the problems of Eastern Europe are rivals for attention, and nearer at hand to the rest of Europe. Furthermore, some argue that growth does not help the poorest in the Third World, and may even hurt them.

The United Nations has published a detailed study of economic development covering one hundred and thirty countries with populations of over one million.[2] It is significant in that it does not deal with the gross national product but tries to measure a human development index, defined as enlarging peoples' chances in terms of freedoms, rights and self-respect. Life-expectancy and literacy, as well as increased purchasing power, then become important. By these criteria eighteen countries came ahead of the USA. Reliance on market forces plays a large part in the various studies, but this is a market which needs careful interventionist policies by the state. There is no suggestion that markets left to themselves will produce the desired result. On the other hand, the survey shows that states have often pursued foolish interventionist policies. In the 1960s and 1970s they often pursued an ideal of self-sufficiency (as much CCPD literature urges!) through protectionist trade policies and heavy state subsidies, instead of promoting trade with the richer states. Energy was subsidized (not good for the environment), and agriculture (in which most of the poor earned their living) quite heavily taxed. There are signs of change now.

Nor does it follow that it is economic growth by the rich world that hinders that of the two-thirds poor world. Much of the Christian comment assumes that it does. Prosperity is not a fixed quantity, so that the growth of the rich sector necessarily takes from the poor. This is the old mercantilist fallacy. No one has prospered because black Africa is getting poorer per head of population, and no country has stayed poor because South Korea and other East Asian countries have grown richer. Whether, of course, the kind of growth is the best, whether in short it is the sustainable growth which the Brundtland Report recommended, is a different question, and one to which we shall return later in this chapter. For the moment let us just stress the importance of international trade for the common good. We shall also have to return to this, after turning from trade to aid.

3. Aid attacked and defended

The governments of relatively wealthy countries are reluctant donors of aid. They do not think that economic aid wins them elections. They are probably right, though there is evidence that sustained campaigning by Christian and secular aid organizations is having some effect, particularly among the younger electorate. The United Nations' target for aid is 0.7% of a state's gross domestic product. The United Kingdom just fails to reach half that, and much of its aid is tied to British exports. The USA is worse. Holland and Sweden have the best records.

However, aid has come under attack from both Right and Left politically. Both say that it props up unpalatable political régimes, whilst the Right adds that it impedes growth by undercutting the market. Lord Peter Bauer, the economist, is particularly associated with this charge. Hong Kong is his ideal. It has 'limited government, a free market, and a population engaged in the single-minded pursuit of making money day and night'.[3] He had argued earlier that economic aid favours tyrannical governments, represses natural entrepreneurial skills, directs resources into military and prestige spending, encourages central planning which then makes a mess of its aims, provides soft options for the governments who receive it, and often inflames international relations because of hidden strings attached to it. As examples, Hong Kong, Singapore and Taiwan have prospered without it, and the phenomenal growth in South Korea's economy in the last thirty years owes little to it.[4]

What is the evidence? A careful study commissioned by the eighteen government members of the Development Committee of the World Bank and the International Monetary Fund appeared in 1987, with a country-by-country analysis.[5] Here are two of its conclusions.

1. Does aid hinder growth? It is unlikely to. In most countries it is only a small factor, and one of many. In India, for example, it has represented only 2–3% of the gross national product, yet it was essential for the 'green revolution', where the use of higher-quality grain has freed India from being at the mercy of monsoons, so that

it has even become an exporter of food. (The political effect of favouring big farmers is another matter.) Where aid has been a bigger factor, as in sub-Saharan Africa, amounting to perhaps half of all investment, it has been in countries where promoting growth is hardest.

2. Does aid take resources from the private sector? Probably not. It is increasingly concerned with the liberalization of trade if it is channelled through multilateral agencies like the World Bank's International Development Association. But too much is tied aid: three-quarters of that from the United Kingdom, two-thirds from the USA, half from Japan, one-third from (West) Germany. Cheap loans are often tied to importing capital goods from the donor country. And donors are apt to preach trade liberalization whilst imposing import duties themselves.

The conclusion is that aid does work in spite of periodic horror stories of waste and mismanagement, but not as well as it should. It is slow, and there is lack of co-ordination by donors.[6] Also, too much goes to middle-income countries, when nearly half the population in less developed countries are below any conceivable definition of *absolute* poverty. How can the relatively affluent tolerate such a scandal?

Every year tens of millions die of hunger or related diseases, and another three to four hundred million do not have enough food to live healthily. In one sense there is nothing new about this. Life has been brutish and short for masses of people throughout history; the difference is that now we know about it globally, and states can tackle it if they will take a global responsibility together. In any case they do react globally, for good or ill.

But before we dwell on that, how far can Third World governments themselves alleviate their situation of chronic hunger and famine? Some countries have almost eliminated chronic hunger, for example, India, Sri Lanka, South Korea and China. To do so involved extensive government public policies on health and education to protect the most vulnerable. Sometimes drastic political measures were needed. In 1990 the leader of the powerful and corrupt Oil Workers' Union in Mexico was jailed, and so were rich tax dodgers. In the same year in Brazil, when prices were rising at 6% per day, four-fifths of savings were suddenly frozen for eighteen months and the government began to abandon the quest for a highly-controlled self-sufficient economy. Inflation can be insidious. In one way Brazil had learned to live with hyper-inflation. Prices were quoted in government bonds whose value was adjusted daily. But the inflation became self-reinforcing as people allowed for it in advance in their calculations. Firms could make more money by financial speculation than by investment; and government finances were destroyed as tax revenues became worth ever less as they came in, so that very high interest rates were charged for borrowing. Whether the Brazilian government has the determination to persist and not weaken in these reforms remains to be seen.

Furthermore, many countries need to curb their population growth. Nigeria has doubled its population since independence to one hundred million, and if this continues to increase at the present rate it will be two hundred million by the year 2000; meanwhile its income per head has fallen by two-thirds in the five years to 1990. But Nigeria is only one example of many countries with the same problem.

Economic and political weaknesses play upon one another. Ethnic and religious conflicts are exacerbated, as in many Asian, sub-Saharan and Middle Eastern countries. Post-colonial days have resulted in many countries with authoritarian, clique-ridden and corrupt governments, more concerned with their own power and patronage than with economic recovery. Incompetence and military indiscipline have combined with bribery and demoralized bureaucracies, together with reliance on an easily organized urban population as against dispersed rural dwellers, to inhibit a wise long-term economic policy. There is no easy way round this. 'Western' insistence on reforms as a condition of aid will provoke charges of neo-colonialism and paternalism. Easing of economic strangleholds may well be the only way in the long run to encourage what cannot be insisted upon. Part of the stranglehold has been restrictions on exports, and higher debt services, and less aid in real terms. A big factor in rising interest rates has been the extent of borrowing by the USA to cover its domestic deficit instead of raising taxes.

So what can the relatively wealthy do? Aid and trade. We have seen that aid can work. What should it promote? There is no lack of suggestions. Health, education, infrastructure to support com-munications necessary for markets, land reforms (most urgent and most resisted in Central and South America), management training, and a development bank to lend to private firms importing raw materials, and for venture capital in general. The more aid is by cash and less in kind the better. Food in a dire emergency is most important, but even then it is better if those in need have money to buy it from private traders, who are likely to get it distributed quickly. And grants are better than loans. Loans involve repayments. We shall turn shortly to questions of debt. But first let us note that trade is even more important than aid.

4. Trade

This brings us at once to the question of cash crops, such as coffee or cocoa. Should Third World agriculture be encouraged to modify its traditional patterns and embark on world trade? Do cash crops compete with food crops for scarce resources, whether fertile land, water, or capital? Growing capital-intensive crops like tobacco and sugar can produce a new class of landless rural proletariat, but growing labour-intensive crops like vegetables can mean that mothers have less time to look after young children, with increasing risks of a rise in infant mortality. There are also hazards of price fluctuations in more distant markets, and the price of food crops may rise more rapidly than their income from cash crops. Questions of sex also enter. Women control the food crops and men the cash crops (and may spend the proceeds on card-playing, bingo and a bicycle rather than on and with their families!). In the Philippines half the population around the sugar mills is now landless (as compared with 10% in subsistence-farming areas), and the wages paid to the landless are very low. It is ominous that the most successful cash crops are drugs.

Yet despite all these hazards, it is hard to believe that with a global economy and increasing population it is possible to keep traditional subsistence-farming unchanged. But if there are to be cash crops, governments must provide a firm infrastructure to sustain them. There is no question of just leaving it to the market. Clean water, basic medical facilities, roads to the markets, fundamental services to cope with cash-flow problems, and advisory information on crops are all necessary. And that gets us back to basic competence in governments and their openness to look beyond the urban population. Very imperfect as the situation is, the evidence is that cash and food crops are not rivals so that it is a case of one or the other, but that they tend to prosper or to falter together.

The importance of trade brings us back to the importance of GATT. Developing countries are usually in a weak power-relationship *vis-à-vis* the developed. They can be bullied; and they can be ignored. They can also have arms thrust at them by forceful sales techniques. They can have their exports discriminated against by the relatively wealthy countries, who want to protect their costly industries or their highly subsidized farmers against competition. The Common Agricultural Policy of the EC is a notorious example, which also encourages over-intensive farming. Wealthy countries do this because they do not have adequate social policies for helping those involved in subsidized production to move out into areas where innovation is needed. So the removal of, for example, protective duties on textiles throws workers in their manufacture out of work and causes them disproportionate hardship, whereas the benefit to the whole country through cheaper imports is widely spread and not so concentrated electorally. How much better it would be if the Third World exported textiles rather than timber! Hence those who talk much of the virtue of competition hinder its working in practice.

GATT provides some check on this. Paradoxically GATT is popular in that twelve countries are wanting to join, including perhaps the USSR and China, and it is preparing to extend its remit to include intellectual property and services (like banking, telecommunications and tourism). On the other hand, those already in GATT have the utmost difficulty in trimming their respective pressure-groups when it comes to negotiating a new agreement. The whole GATT structure may break down, with a lapse into short-sighted protectionism. If this happens, it will be a disaster for the Third World and a disgrace to the statesmanship of the First World countries. It is vital that the Third World has access to the markets of the First World, and that the First World does not try to be self-sufficient and use its skills to devise import substitutions instead of trading with the Third World. GATT has the advantage that small countries can at least appeal to the accepted rules if large countries infringe them, which is some protection (although far from complete) against being bullied; and this although the GATT system has largely benefited the rich, especially the USA, the EC and Japan, and despite the fact that decisions are taken by consensus. Power realities cannot be eliminated, though they can be weakened.

The limitations of GATT should not cause it to be condemned; any alternative at the moment which has a possibility of implementation would be worse. At the least, the seventy or more developing countries are allowed to curb imports and subsidize exports (when the rest are not), without offering anything in return. (Whether they are usually wise to do so is another matter.) Nor does GATT insist on any particular ownership, private or public, of factors of production, so long as the price reflects the cost of buying and selling in response to the market. It could not work easily with the collapsed Soviet-style command economies.

5. Debt

That countries should borrow is not new. All the newly industrializing countries in the nineteenth century borrowed heavily. Problems arise if the volume of debt becomes too great as a percentage of the national income. If it gets high, the proportion of foreign exchange earned that is needed for interest payments becomes unbearable. Argentina is said to need 130% of its export earnings to service its debts! Debt is made worse if trading goes on in a range of currencies of which the most powerful one rises in value against the rest. This has happened to the American dollar in recent years.

The most important debts are loans from governments to governments, on either a bilateral or multilateral basis. They are usually long-term (perhaps a decade), at fairly low interest, and in principle renegotiable. Bank loans are harder to renegotiate, and are for a shorter term. Some of the present troubles are due to the efforts of banks to recycle the oil revenues of the oil-rich states after the price rise of 1973–4. The International Monetary Fund also lends to governments (usually with conditions attached). These loans are short-term and expensive. Sometimes suppliers of goods also lend to purchasers, but these loans are very short-term, costly and inflexible.

There is no easy way out of the problems these international debts have created. Clearly grants, especially to the poorest countries, do not present such problems. Clearly also, loans can be written off, and a percentage should be. But mutuality in international trade relations needs to grow, and loans are properly part of this.

That is why reneging on loans, as Peru, Brazil and Mexico have partially done, or threatened to do, is not a long-term solution. It would deny these countries future loans, and their governments would have to inflict a ferocious rate of forced saving on their citizens to secure necessary capital resources (as the Russian government did from soon after 1917). That would almost certainly mean totalitarian governments, and that is not in the interests of any country, First or Third World.

Moreover, governments who borrow need to use their resources wisely. Much of the post-1974 bank loans were squandered on recurrent items rather than capital projects. International Monetary Fund and World Bank loans are more monitored, but that creates resentment and charges of neo-colonialism and paternalism. It is IMF prescriptions which are charged with being insensitive, and particularly onerous in their effects on the poorest. Everything is easier if the First World will trade with the Third World. We come back again and again to that.

6. *Economic growth, ecological issues and the environment*

So far ecological and environmental issues have scarcely been mentioned. Economic growth has been affirmed as a necessity for the Third World, and it has been suggested that a continuation of it in the First World will be a help and not a hindrance to the Third World *if* it is sustainable in itself and wise in its priorities. This is what the Brundtland Report advocated.[7] Is such growth feasible or is it contradictory? There has been an explosion of discussion on these issues.

The twenty-four countries of the OECD, which include the USA, Western Europe, Japan, Australia and New Zealand, contain 16% of the world's population and produce 72% of its gross domestic production. They have 78% of the world's road vehicles, use 50% of its energy, and import 73% of its forest products. They have been creating more pollution and more waste, consuming more natural resources like oil, water and wood, and degrading the soil by salination and the use of pesticides. The only improvement they have made in recent years is some reduction in the amount of sulphur dioxide produced by acid rain, and the production of the Montreal Protocol of 1989 restricting the use of chlorofluorocarbons. Clearly, changes must be made to ensure that the life-support systems of the planet are not endangered. Economic growth must be 'cleaner'. Natural resources need to be safeguarded, the environment needs protection from health hazards, waste must be minimized, energy used more efficiently in its own terms rather than in the economic sense of efficiency, and all this done by the co-operation of national sovereign states. For hazards such as ozone depreciation and climatic changes are global. Nor can the market be left to deal with these issues, for it will not cope with externalities, nor the free-rider problem, and will not take a long enough view (as we have already seen in Chapter 2). Every country has an interest in cheating, especially as the regional impact of global warming is not clear, and some areas will probably benefit from it. The political task is daunting; it is a further example of the challenge to human beings to a responsible use of their intelligence, reason and will, in this case in relation to nature.

Yet while, for example, checks on the output of carbon dioxide will slow the global growth of the world's gross product (perhaps by up to 0.5% p.a.), it will not prevent growth. Here another difficulty arises. The developing countries will suffer most by such checks, and yet their co-operation is essential. If a tax per person on carbon emissions above a certain point were levied, Third World countries would be hit hardest. The primary responsibility must lie with the First World countries. They must pursue policies which will reduce carbon emissions, by taxation or tradeable permits, and then compensate those who lose most, that is Third World countries. That brings us back to aid by grants and subsidies.

At this point, there is a challenge by much more radical ecologists in the 'Western' world who regard the whole Brundtland approach as patent nonsense. Some want to subsume human beings in nature, and regard the effort to make a distinction between humans and the rest of nature as arrogance.[8] There is TOES (The Other Economic Summit). It has the same concern as Brundtland for conservation of the environment, the sustainable use of resources, and the satisfaction of basic human needs the world over, but argues for self-reliance on the part of each state. Each should rely primarily on its own strength in terms of its natural and cultural environment. A transformation is needed in social relationships, economic activities and power structures in favour of self-management in decision-making; a revolution from below is needed in terms of the common sense and common values of ordinary people; active solidarity is to be the motivating force. In particular, developing nations are to use their usually adequate resources on what their people need rather than for the export market, whilst the rich countries should cut their production until they use only one-fifth of the resources they use now.[9]

This thinking has many echoes in recent ecumenical productions from the WCC. Perhaps enough has been said in this book to suggest how fanciful most of it is, politically as well as economically. Levels of consumption among the world's poor areas will never rise to what we could regard as a reasonable level without investment; and the investment cannot be provided from within. That brings us back once more to trade and aid.[10] Resources thus gained need to be spent, as we have seen, on an appropriate infrastructure, but also on an appropriate (i.e. less elaborate) technology for farmers, and to raise levels of productivity among the unskilled workers. Wise economic growth, wisely administered, is needed in the world generally to promote these aims.

7. Summary

Suspicion of economic and technological development as such is misplaced. It makes possible an escape from dire poverty. Most people still suffer from poor diet, housing and health care. Even a country highly developed in these respects, the USA, has many millions in relative poverty, including the scandal of thirty-five millions without health care. So the wealthy countries have to look to what they do with their resources, and especially with increased growth. The less developed need to take up appropriate (sometimes called intermediate) technology, and be helped by the rich to do this. Strong national and international governmental policies are needed, and we are only at the beginning of the latter and are lukewarm about the former. If the United Nations can raise a levy for a peace force, let it raise one for aid, trade and environmental issues. The market left to itself cannot cope.

However messy political activity is, denigration of politics is also misplaced. Trade policies which accept imports from the Third World involve active domestic social policies to cushion and retrain those displaced, and thereby reduce trade union antagonism. For Third World countries to shut themselves into a kind of self-sufficiency behind tariffs, quotas and other barriers to imports, ignoring world prices, may be understandable in terms of the power relationships between them and the First World, but it would keep them in a poverty ghetto and produce staggering economic inefficiency. Can the power base of the Third World be strengthened? It is urgent that it should be. It was done with one commodity: oil. What other possibilities are there?[11] One is that it can bargain about the greenhouse effect. All the efforts of other countries to reduce ozone depreciation by reducing or banning the use of chlorofluorocarbons (CFCs) will be nullified if India and China do not co-operate. And why should Brazilian peasants bother about the greenhouse effect if they can only stay alive by burning the rain forests? The wealthy world must pay them to co-operate and pay them to stop. The wealthy themselves must check their own waste and pollution, using market mechanisms as much as possible and coercive legislation beyond that.

Wealth-creation is a vocation, a response to a God-given possibility. What is done with it is a separate human responsibility. A prospect of ever-rising individual (and family) consumption accompanied by corporate squalor and widening divisions between rich and poor has nothing to be said for it. In creating wealth, economic efficiency is an important criterion, and all the more important because it is so often overlooked or misunderstood. It makes us alert to the avoidance of waste. But economic efficiency is not the only criterion. Appeals to the 'enterprise culture' need to be heard with caution. It is possible to give the term a plausible meaning if 'enterprise' stands for the avoidance of economic waste and for a general alertness to changing factors which the market fosters. But when 'culture' is added to enterprise, doubts arise. Enterprise as widely understood is precisely not what we want as an overall cultural criterion. It leads to short-term managerial criteria being brought to bear in public areas like education, housing, health care, the social services and the arts, to an extent far beyond their appropriate place.

Lastly, how far can an appeal be made to altruism in international relations with respect to the responsibilities of the affluent? Mrs Brundtland has said: 'You cannot breathe the air and you cannot be secure without caring for others who are doing the same thing.' Alas, you can! States always act from what they consider to be their self interest,[12] except for short periods and in dire emergencies. Unless this is accepted, we live in a world of illusion.

The problem is to persuade states where their long-term interest lies. The Brandt Reports did their best to do this,[13] but so far with little result. But there is no other way. Efforts must go on being made to put this case. Public awareness is increasing all the time. The effort to deal with chlorofluorocarbons came quite quickly when the politicians realized the problem.

The root issue is this: can the First World (and the Second, come to that) be content to pursue its own present economic and environmental policies and shut itself in a kind of ghetto isolated from the Third World? To say that they cannot is an appeal to altruism. Is it feasible to make such an appeal and ally this appeal with the appeal to self-interest? Perhaps to a very limited and temporary extent, votes can be moved mainly by altruism, and we should not neglect the appeal to it.[14] But for a long-term pull on many issues it is the self-interest argument that has to prove its cogency. Christians should see the importance of their contribution to presenting it, thereby helping to make its implementation an electoral possibility, and not a hindrance to governments in pursuing long-term policies.

Epilogue

A book which began with an overview does not need an extensive epilogue, but some things had better be added, partly to recall its central theme, partly to place it in the present theological context. To begin with there is the word 'ambiguity'. In customary use it has several shades of meaning, some rather derogatory. Or, less adversely, it can refer to an inherent uncertainty in meaning, or to something not as clearly expressed, as it might be. None of these senses quite fits my purpose. I use 'ambiguity' to refer to the analysis of a phenomenon which has an important and valid aspect but which at the same time has aspects, inseparable from what is valuable, which are undesirable. A popular expression of these would be 'trade-offs'. I apply 'ambiguity' to capitalism, not to the doctrinal expressions of Christian faith.[1] Christian doctrine has a 'both-and' aspect, the necessity of holding in tension two facets of reality, like grace and freedom, or dignity and sinfulness in relation to human persons, both of which will always characterize human life. In respect to particular social institutions like capitalism, though, it is possible at least in theory to benefit from the positive side and erect a counter-balance to the negative side.

In the economic realm, I have written in the context of the collapse of the Soviet-style economies to urge the necessity of taking the market seriously as the only alternative on offer to deal with fundamental economic problems which any society has to solve. It is a sophisticated human invention. To appreciate the market it is necessary to understand the basic assumptions which underlie economics. Lacking this understanding, the citizen finds it hard to make wise judgments. He or she can be misled by the special pleading of vested interests, not realizing the economic cost, in terms of alternatives foregone, of what they advocate. There is nothing inherently wrong with vested interests. Persons and groups have their own experience which others do not share to the same extent. It is right that they should express it in the public forum.

But others have their interests, which also need to be heard. It is not easy for persons, and still less for groups, to transcend their own perspective and realize that there are other legitimate interests than their own, and that some tolerable adjustment must be made between them. It is debates in the public forum which assist this process, rough and ready as it usually is. It is unwise to have a fear of the political log-rolling of vested interests, and contrast it with the purity of the impersonal market, ignoring the power relations behind that, and the controls needed to prevent abuses.[2]

The serious limitations of the market have been obscured by a great deal of New Right propaganda in the last twenty years. The market cannot cope by itself with the many problems mentioned in this book, though it can make, and needs to make, a contribution to dealing with them. The need is to move to politics, within which the contribution of economics will find its place.

When it comes to a Christian social theology, it is clear that there is little support for the philosophy of possessive individualism associated with the political philosophy of the New Right.[3] This may well, however, still be popular in the pews, especially in Protestantism, because of the individualist spectacles through which the Bible and Christian doctrine has been seen in the centuries of Protestant culture since the rise of capitalism. This is indeed a triumph of capitalism.

A preoccupation of this book is the concern for the tools that are necessary to bring the data of the Bible and doctrine to bear on the modern world. Adequate analysis of 'what is going on' requires an element of expertise, hence our concern with the use and limits of economics. But expertise by itself cannot settle anything, even if all the experts agree, which is rarely the case. Finally, it comes down to personal judgments, individually or corporately, ideally made with an informed conscience. Guidance at a middle level may help, but when it comes to detailed implementation there is likely to be a range of choices, except in extreme circumstances. Conscientious Christians will be found making different choices. Those who are unwilling to admit the ambiguities in human life do not like this. They want a clear Christian choice in ethical issues. They forget the difficulty of ethical reasoning; even if there is agreement on basic values from a Christian perspective, there is the problem of selecting and evaluating relevant 'facts', of relevant expertise, and of the personal and social ideological interests which affect judgments. The more these can be transcended the better, but it is not possible completely to transcend them.[4]

This is obviously a book from the First World. The Second, or Marxist, world is scarcely involved in it, because it is in such disarray that it is hard to know what to say of it at the moment. But in the end it will be involved – sooner, we must hope, rather than later. Meanwhile, a debate is needed between the position of this book and those in the Third World. The First World has badly misused its power in respect of the Third World. Where it has done good things it has paid itself well. But it has a sad record of atrocities, notably in the slave trade, and in genocide. In the twentieth century it has involved the Third World in two world wars, neither of which was of its making; and since the end of the second one it has been mean in its economic attitude to the Third World. Clearly repentance is called for. How, for instance, was 1992 celebrated, not only in Europe with its Common Market, but in Latin America?[5] In ecumenical circles the First World is becoming aware of this. Then a new danger looms.

The danger arises because it is only too easy for the Third World to ascribe all its misfortunes to the First World.[6] I fear that if this book is read in the Third World it will be dismissed as a product of the wealthy and privileged 'West'. But I hope we may have got to the stage of mutual correction, where my arguments are assessed on their merits, not dismissed because of the country from which they come; and I am open to criticism from those whose position enables them to see things from a different perspective from mine. As I see it, what I have written about the importance and limitations of economics, and the need for an adequate political economy, applies globally. The vast increase of productivity since the agricultural and industrial revolutions has brought great blessings, but was accompanied by much ruthlessness and injustice. Can we use the present explosion of productivity without similar ruthlessness, primarily to banish the crippling poverty of so much of the Third World? And can we do so in an environmentally sustainable way? From the First World this requires more than better trade and aid policies; it also requires better domestic policies and a deeper philosophy of social relationships than capitalism left to itself conceives. The Third World has also its responsibilities to face. In the public forum in both, cogent arguments need to be produced on the basis of the long-term interests of each state to back up the fitful and often ephemeral (though important) element of altruism which human beings are capable of feeling for their fellow humans.

Moreover there are some emphases in the theological scene today which I consider unhelpful. They are found in Britain, but more strongly elsewhere. (The British temptation is the reverse of what I am about to mention; it is an attachment to accepted ways.) One tendency is a fondness for what is called an action-reflection method of working. It is a legacy of Marx's insistence in the eleventh of his theses on Feuerbach (1845): 'The philosophers have only *interpreted* the world, in various ways; the point, however, is to change it.' The favoured word is orthopraxis. The action-reflection model wants to break away from a 'pure' theology, allegedly unaffected by any cultural factors (but in fact unavowedly ideologically slanted), which is then 'applied' to current ethical issues. Rather, it is held, there should be action first, not merely commitment to action, particularly for and with the poor; after that comes reflection. In this way Christians will change the world and not merely reflect on it. The trouble with this is that the action may well be mistaken, or not the best possible, because of the lack of an adequate analysis of the situation. Action and reflection should not be thought of as a fixed sequence, or polarized one against the other, but be thought of as reciprocally related.

Another tendency is for theologians to want to say something with force about the world today, and then find various escape routes from dealing with its realities. They are impatient with the ambiguities which would be disclosed if they did encounter the realities. One route is to denounce the many evils of today from the perspective of an ideal expression of the kingdom of God in the world, and then arrive at a few very tepid proposals when it comes to recommending some action to deal with the enormities which they have denounced. We have had an example of this in Moltmann,[7] who has been criticized (with others) by liberation theologians for it. Another habit, perhaps less common than twenty years ago, is to demand a total reconstruction of the social and political order, and to add that nothing can be said on what should replace it until the old order has been destroyed.

A third line, becoming more popular now, is to abandon the large-scale issues of public policy and government and take refuge in local communities, churchly and secular. This approach is based on a kind of apocalyptic radicalism. Apocalyptic thought was widely current in Judaism among the less orthodox at the time of Jesus. We have examples of it in both Testaments, the chief being the book of Daniel in the Old Testament and the book of Revelation in the New Testament. In brief, it held that the world was going from bad to worse in the hands of the ungodly, and would continue to do so until God intervened to clear things up, either on this earth, or on a new one. God is sovereign over past, present and future. The faithful can only hang on in expectation of God's triumph, although it might mean their martyrdom.[8]

Efforts to reassert the relevance of apocalyptic for today are not very convincing; and as a tactic, the concentration on the small community, congregation or commune is an evasion of responsibility. There is certainly a place for such communities; perhaps where Christians are a small minority, but not necessarily even there. Christians form about 1% of the Japanese population, but this does not seem an obviously wise or necessary strategy there. Where Christians are more numerous, and where they have responsibilities in working and civic life, as workers and citizens, they should not concentrate their vision on a local Christian group to such an extent as not to work with others in the body politic, who may well base their life on some other faith or philosophy, but have similar social goals in a current context. Those who stress an apocalyptic hope urge us to anticipate God's new age now, and live now as if it were here, in new communities based on the imitation of Christ. Some may indeed be called to live some kind of communal life, whether in a religious order or not, but I have not seen any clear account of how such a vision bears upon the urgent issues discussed in this book. I think it is an evasion of responsibility.

The kingdom of God is not solely in the future. Since the ministry of Jesus it is already working as leaven in the world; or, putting it another way, the Spirit is co-operating for good in human life with all who are striving witin its ambiguities to create relative structures of justice, which will operate more humanely than the present ones, whilst preserving what may be good from the past. Creation, preservation and change are intertwined. We shall be living with ambiguities until the end of time. We need to do so creatively and with courage. What new things in God's providence may face humanity we do not know. Since we cannot know them, they cannot be the basis of decisions now. Neverthe-less, all our decisions are made in a firm hope for the final fulfilment of God's good purposes, of which we already have a foretaste through Jesus Christ.[9]

Appendices

every time the seventh year of release is at hand, for there will always be poor: 'the poor will never cease out of the land.' Other passages in the Old Testament say substantially the same thing (Lev. 25.35–38; Deut. 23.19f.; Neh. 5.9–11; Ezek. 18.5–20), whilst Psalm 15.5 says that one requirement for being acceptable to God is not having put one's money out to usury. The Old Testament is addressing a people who regarded themselves as specially related to God, with whom he had made a covenant. In our terms they were a church. The Torah, or Law, was an effort to bring the idea of the covenant to bear on the social situation of the time, in order to express in the structures of society the concept of social justice and harmony, summed up in the rich term *shalom* which we rather inadequately translate by the word peace. Hence, although high interest rates were common in the Babylonian and Near Eastern culture of the time, the Old Testament forbids this among members of the covenant community.

The New Testament does not contain such prohibitions. The legal context of Jesus' ministry was a Roman one which had a maximum rate of interest of 12%, and contemporary language tended to call a greater rate of interest than this usury. Incidentally, the New Testament assumes that lending at interest is going on, but makes no mention of an ethic of interest as such. The parable of the talents in Matthew 25 has the owner saying to the recipient of the one talent who has buried it for safety so that he could return it to the donor intact, 'You wicked and slothful servant ... you ought to have invested my money with bankers, and at my coming I should have received what was my own with interest' (vv. 26f.). On the other hand, Luke 6.35 in the Vulgate version was to have a great influence. In the RSV it reads 'lend, expecting nothing in return', with a textual variant 'despairing of no man'. The Vulgate reads 'lend, hoping for nothing thence', which was interpreted as meaning that loans should be free of interest. On this basis a whole series of councils of the church condemned the taking of interest by clergy or laity (Arles 314, Nicaea 325, Carthage 345, the Second Council of Lyons 1127, The Third Lateran Council 1179, Vienna 1311). It was because of this that Christians used Jews for borrowing, and they justified themselves on the basis of Deuteronomy 15, already quoted, or 23.20: 'To a foreigner you may lend upon interest, but to your brother you shall not lend.' This proved profitable to both parties. Indeed money-lending was so profitable to the Jews that they could easily cope with the provision in England and France that half of their property should go to the king when they died.

The New Testament also contains cryptic references to the so-called 'communism' of the early church in Jerusalem (Acts 2.43–47;

4.32–37). It appears to have been a voluntary pooling of, and living on, capital in anticipation of the imminent *parousia* or return of Christ. When this did not happen the church had impoverished itself, and St Paul spent a good deal of his time in arranging for a collection in his Gentile churches for the poor mother church in Jerusalem. Indeed it was a visit there to hand it over that led to his arrest.

The working out of an ethic of finance, however, followed upon the rediscovery of Artistotle. His teaching comes as part of a section in the *Politics* expressing opposition to all pecuniary gains from commercial transactions. He says 'money was intended to be used in exchange not to increase usury' (*Works*, Vol. 10, 1256b–1258b, trans. B. Jowett). Usury is the unnatural breeding of money for money. 'Nature' makes each separate thing for a separate end, and its use for any other end is contrary to nature, and improper. The proper end of money is as a means of exchange; lending at interest is therefore an improper use.

The mediaeval church tried to work out the implications of this teaching in a society which began to be on the move as merchant capitalism developed in the Italian city states, and where loans were not so much for consumption by those in a temporary emergency as for productive purposes. There was a theological quest for an economic policy based on an understanding of the nature of man in the setting of nature as a whole, using reason in the interests of justice. The problem was how to legitimize a productive loan without infringing the basic assumption of the barrenness of money and of the illegitimacy of making a charge for the use of it. In doing this the church faced the internal obstacle of a traditional society, including a financial aristocracy, which was reluctant to allow the flexibility that trade required.

Usury was by far the most debated and the most important economic issue in moral theology. In other economic matters the church accepted what the civil law allowed. Its differentiation of the counsels of perfection from the precepts binding on all Christian allowed a minority to opt out of the moral ambiguities of economic life, or so they thought, into religious communities. On usury, however, the church produced its own detailed teaching, discriminating precisely between licit and illicit contracts. On the question of the just price, for instance, by the seventeenth century the schoolmen came, without too much difficulty, to agree that it was the market price. The value of an article lies in the common human demand for it (though this is not necessarily the same as human need).

On the question of money the teaching depended on a distinction, going back to Roman law, between fungible and non-fungible goods. Fungible ones lose their identity in use; they are transformed or destroyed. Wine is an example. Non-fungible ones are not, as for instance in leasing or renting. Money was treated as fungible. Money could be loaned but not leased. If a house is leased the same house is returned to the owner at the expiration of the lease. If money is leased the same coins cannot be returned because they have been destroyed or transformed in being spent by the borrower. Moreover time is a free gift of God, so it is usurious to make a charge for the use of money over time; in the case of a *mutuum*, or loan, the borrower was to return the amount of the money lent, whereas the obligation to pay an annual return on fruitful property like land (the *census*) caused no difficulty.

How in terms of such teaching could a productive loan in which there was some risk to the lender be justified? Three justifications were developed.

1. The concept of *damnum energens*; the lender could charge for a loan if it turned out that he suffered economic damage by lending, especially if the loan was not repaid on time.
2. The concept of *lucrum cessans*; this is compensation for surrendering the possibility of gain which the lender might have made if he himself had had the use of the money lent.
3. The concept of *societas* or partnership; in this the partner retains control of his own money. This proved the basis of much capitalist risk-bearing or entrepreneurship in the late Middle Ages. Notice that it implicitly calls into question the doctrine of the sterility of money on which the basic teaching against usury was based.

The only formal exception made by the moralists to this basic teaching concerned the establishment of *montes pietatis*, or public pawnshops, approved by the Lateran Council of 1515. These were run for the poor and not for profit; they were financed by charitable donations, and made a small charge of 6% for the costs of administration at a time when usurers would charge from 32% to 43%. It was their establishment that led to the belief that banking could indeed be a livelihood, and thus to the beginning of legitimizing a structure of institutional banking.

The church continued to maintain the teaching that usury meant profit on a formal loan contract. Intense debates continued among the moral theologians and canonists. Molina, Lugo and Lessius, with writings on right and justice, were the chief contributors in the seventeenth century. Rather than abandon usury and the presuppositions on which it rested, the church allowed it to be interpreted narrowly and legalistically, and by what amounted to legal fictions.

Thus there was greater willingness to recognize the legitimacy, honesty and social utility of financiers.

The need to find a legitimate basis for business finance was the impetus to the theoretical discussion. In particular the application of the concept of insurance to the contracts in a *societas*, thus allowing for risks, implied a further rejection in practice of the idea of the sterility of money. So Viner can say that moral theology at the end of the seventeenth century was formally the same in substance as at the end of the thirteenth.[1] It was frozen and lifeless. Reverenced in seminaries, it lost all influence in the outside world. And it was increasingly replaced by secular moral philosophy, and in Protestant countries by a nationalistic mercantilism. Secular economic literature dates from the end of the seventeenth century.

The basic scholastic teaching on usury was reiterated by Alexander VII in 1666 and Innocent XI in 1679. The last papal treatment was directed to Italy by Benedict XIV in 1745, and universalized by the Holy Office in 1835. In practice the interest allowed by law was sanctioned. References to usury in the encyclical *Rerum Novarum* of 1891, which made a new start in papal social teaching, are unclear, and the Canons of 1917 give the presumption to the legal rate of interest, whilst holding that it is possible that it may be excessive, or usurious in the modern use of the term. The traditional teaching had faded out. More and more it smacked of sophistry in finding roundabout ways of justifying interest, and its endemic inconsistencies were becoming ever more obvious. The veto on a loan of money over time (apart from the question of risk) was never rationally established; the theory that risk went with ownership was contradicted when insurance was declared legitimate; and the conviction that money was sterile was called in question by the concept of the *societas*. However, the teaching was formally maintained, with the result that the paradox that the charge for money to a profit-seeking borrower must depend on the circumstances of the lender was never faced. The insight the just price theory had arrived at, that value is determined by supply and subjective wants, was not applied to money. Pure interest was the enemy, a fixed payment stipulated in advance, which was certain whether or not the borrower gained by it; time was not an economic factor.[2]

Why was this? Partly it was due to treating the Vulgate translation of Luke 6.35 as a rule for economic life. Much more was due to an uncritical acceptance of a natural law doctrine going back to Aristotle. It was perhaps not surprising that before the period of rapid social and economic change following the Industrial Revolution the assumption was that nature is fixed, and that the human aspects of it are no exception. St Paul made this mistake in connection with the length of men's and women's hair (I Cor. 11.14ff). In fact human beings impart a dynamism to nature, and the legitimacy of what they may do can only be evaluated by criteria which derive from basic theological or philosophical presumptions brought alongside empirical investigations of what is going on, or proposed. These need to use concepts from the natural and social sciences which are relevant to the enquiry. This allows a certain autonomy to these sciences. In the case of economic life it means using the concept of the market as one means of allocating scarce resources, and the role of capital in allocating them between consumption goods and various possible productive investments; interest is then the price of waiting instead of spending the money lent.[3]

Traditional moral theology made the same mistake about nature in other spheres and, where it has not been reformed, still does. The encyclical *Humanae Vitae* uses three not entirely compatible arguments against contraception, one of them depending on the assumption that it is clear that human genital organs are naturally designed for reproduction, and therefore any use of them in coitus which is not apt for reproduction is unnatural.

To return to the question of usury. Why was Aristotle canonized by Christians? There are two possible reasons. One is that he was assumed to be empirically correct. That is to say, the church was following the best expertise of the day. If this is the reason, it is a hazard which constantly besets Christian thinkers. In the economic field many of them uncritically accepted in the depression following the 1929 Wall Street crash the social credit monetary theories of the engineer Major Douglas. In this case they were culpable because they did not trouble to master the economic tools which would have enabled them to appraise the theories.

More recently, many accepted uncritically the first of the Club of Rome Reports, *The Limits to Growth* (1972), the theoretical base of which was equally unsound.[4] A third example is the proneness of the liberation theologians of Latin America to take over Marxist social and economic analyses and assume that they are 'scientifically' correct.[5] There is no escaping the problems of empirical investigation, and of evaluating rival theories and rival expertise. The church can do no more than be alert to these hazards, since it cannot escape them; but it needs to take care not to invest so much authority in any one analysis that it cannot bring itself to abandon the analysis when the evidence is overwhelmingly against it. This the church did in its adoption of Aristotle on usury. The other reason for canonizing his view was that it was thought to be rationally self-evident without the need of empirical investigation, an attitude more easy to adopt when social change was slow and when loans were overwhelmingly for consumption. Hence also the assumption that biblical texts on usury could be translated directly into contemporary practice. Traditional church teaching on doctrine and ethics has all been formulated against this background of assumed stability. Some still cling to it in spite of the experience of the last two centuries. Liturgies are still locked in it. The authority attached to the *magisterium* in the Roman Catholic Church has made the task of moral theology particularly difficult; it has been hard to move for fear of admitting error. This has been the case with slavery and religious liberty, as well as usury, and the situation persists at the moment in the case of several questions of sexual ethics.

What of Protestantism? Luther preached two sermons on usury, in 1519 and in 1520, in which he was more rigorous than the moral theologians, and appealed to the doctrine of canon law unsoftened by the qualifications of the later jurists. He took Luke 6.35 literally, to the extent of condemning rent and a traffic in annuities. Soon he became so alarmed at the Peasants' Revolt that he modified his teaching. Interest, he now said, should be regulated not by the gospel but by the current economic situation and in terms of public utility (*Tract on Trade and Usury*, 1524). Later still, in 1539, he thought that the question of interest should be settled by the Princes and by individual conscience; he himself thought 8% legitimate. Nothing directly useful can be gained from Luther, whose economic utterances were aptly described by R.H. Tawney as 'the occasional explosions of a capricious volcano'.[6] However in the doctrine of the two realms, which lies behind his later utterances, there is the seed of an important insight: that there is an autonomy of the different areas of knowledge; that theology cannot be the queen of the sciences in the traditional way; and that in economics, for example, the layman cannot be told what to do and what not to do and what to think by ecclesiastical persons on some *a priori* deductive basis not arising out of investigation of the area in question.

With Calvin we are in a different world. He attacked the Aristotelian and scholastic concept of the sterility of money. Only money left in a money box is sterile; borrowed for productive purposes it is fruitful (*Sermon 28* on Deut. 23.18–20). The Old Testament prohibitions belong to the Jewish economy. Land and capital are interchangeable as investments, so that interest is as ethically justifiable as rent. The Mosaic rule and the gospel injunction are to be expressed in society in the light of 1. the individual conscience, 2. the Golden Rule, and 3. the principle of public utility; in short, as part of the general problem of social relations within the Christian community. We are not to show harshness to the needy. Usury should not be taken from the poor, or exceed the legal limit, nor should the lender make a greater profit than the borrower (*De Usuris*). Calvin had no intention of being lax in social requirements. He had a lively antagonism to avarice, and handled monetary phenomena with some suspicion. He condemned making one's living as a usurer. Usurers should be expelled from the church. But taking and making an occasional loan for business purposes was not against God's will. Psalm 15.5 was to be interpreted according to the norm of charity and equity. In practice a Geneva church ordinance of 1541 allowed interest of 5%, raising it to 6.7% in 1557.

Clearly this is an interim position, on the way to a secular theory of the market. But the basis of it was a break both from a literal attitude to the Bible and from traditional natural law doctrine. In Britain, Calvinist moral theologians in the next century, like Ames near the beginning of it and Baxter near the end, were to continue to reason within these parameters. But the framework could not be maintained. By the end of the seventeenth century it had collapsed. As early as 1571 in England an Act distinguished between usury and interest, and legalized the latter up to 10%. It said that even a rate less than this could not be enforced if the borrower jibbed at it, but that was a dead letter. If borrowers wanted a facility of borrowing they had to pay interest.[7]

No more was heard of the traditional doctrine after the beginning of the eighteenth century. A nationalist mercantilism replaced it, whose concern with interest was with its role, not its legitimacy. Blackstone in 1776 could say without any fear of contradiction that the total prohibition of usury came from a time of 'monkish superstition and civil tyranny', and that a credit economy and loans upon interest were owed to the 'revival of true religion and real liberty' in the Reformation (*Commentaries* 2, ch. 30). It was of this whole enterprise that Tawney said that 'the Church ceased to count because she ceased to think',[8] whilst Noonan's verdict strikes a different note in saying that 'the long history of usury theory is filled with controversies in which asperity more than charity has distinguished the disputants'.[9]

2. It is not an encouraging story. The church was quite right to be concerned with economic and financial issues. The bases on which it operated were the trouble. The concept of natural law is an important one, though its name is misleading, because its importance is to stress that the realm of the moral is natural to human beings. That is to say that the capacity to recognize that there are moral distinctions, and to

bring that recognition to bear on particular ethical decisions, is one of the distinguishing attributes by which we identify a *human* being as distinct from other animate creatures. But it does not provide the basis for a direct conclusion about the naturalness or otherwise of a particular social phenomenon or institution. Some intermediate steps, involving empirical investigations, are necessary. Similarly, one cannot make such a move from a biblical text. Its detailed prescriptions are related to the historical situation out of which they came. Yet Christians are continually prone to reason as if they were not, for example in the questions of divorce or homosexuality. They did for centuries in the case of slavery, for a strong biblical case in favour of it can be made. It has now been given up. In the field of finance Calvin handled the biblical text flexibly. But those in the Reformed tradition have not always done so. In practice, attempts to read off detailed requirements for a social order from the text of the Bible are highly selective. The Old Testament law-codes, particularly Leviticus, are drawn upon, but not the 'communism' of Acts.

A recent example is a book by Alan Storkey,[10] which has interesting things to say about the economic order, but its basis is unsatisfactory. It attacks economics on the ground that factual, empirical knowledge is a delusion, thus denying any element of autonomy to economics, when in fact at a certain level economics has its own sphere of study, equally applicable to, for example, the Soviet, the Swedish or the American economy. Storkey argues that all knowledge involves commitments of faith and belief, which is true in that it presupposes that the universe is intelligible and not a chaos; but from this he makes the jump to the assertion that we need a revelation, thus removing at one stroke the entire level of human life in a plural world covered by the natural law doctrine; there can be no autonomy for economics: each religion and philosophy will have its own brand.

We are given some general reflections drawn from Leviticus, whose laws are said to be in aid of human independence, on usury in the Old Testament (with the suggestion that unpaid debts today should be cancelled after seven years), and then some wise words on the need to deal with institutional structures and not be content with an ethic only for individuals. But the basis for doing so turns out to be no more specific than the commandment to love our neighbour as ourselves, for instance in large-scale capital markets.[11] This neighbourly rule of God for right living is to be substituted for short-sightedness and self-interest.[12] There are then seven pages of detailed proposals,[13] such as a progressive wealth tax of 3% in favour of the young, and the prohibition of closed shops, but they are not argued for, and no connection is made between them and the Bible on which stress is laid elsewhere in the book. We need to know how to move from the commandment to love our neighbour to such proposals.

It is these middle steps about which Christian social theology has been confused. The Pastoral Letter of the Roman Catholic bishops in the USA on its economy provides another interesting example of the problem.[14] Although they intend to speak to the whole nation, and not only to Roman Catholics or only to Christians, the bishops have abandoned a natural law basis for a biblical one. To this they add traditional church social teaching – which they gloss as much more uniform and relevant than it has in fact been – together with rational reflection on the realities of economic life. However, from the Bible they do build up some rich perceptions which can provide criteria in evaluating ethical issues. The basic one is the dignity of the human person in community. If someone were to suggest that this seems to stem more from the Enlightenment than from the Bible, as traditionally interpreted, I should reply that the Enlightenment made the church alert to evils it had ignored or played down, and to attitudes it needed to cultivate, and that any tendency among Christians to denigrate the Enlightenment is to be deplored until we are sure that we have learned from it all that we need to. I think the interpretation of the bishops can be sustained. From this basic criterion they arrive at three concepts: 1. *Creation*, which leads to the stewardship of created resources by humans under God; 2. *Covenant*, which expands from one covenant people in the Old Testament to include in principle all humanity in the New; 3. *Community*, involving care for one's neighbour: this includes justice for the neighbour, which is measured socially in particular by the treatment of the poor and the powerless. These three concepts are filled out in some detail, and from them the bishops go on to discuss three priority principles: 1. the need to fulfil the basic necessities of the poor; 2. the increased participation of the marginalized in society should have preference over the privileged in power and wealth; 3. there should be a priority for investment in human needs as against luxury and military goods.

Whatever we may think of these general statements, when we come to the specific proposals of the bishops they do not get to grips with the mechanism of running an economic order. They do not analyse the basic economic problem of resource allocation, what to produce and when; and whether or how far to distribute according to the criteria of right, or merit, or need. Nor do they discuss the philosophy which is commonly attached to the market economy, and compare it with their own criteria.

We may appear to have wandered some way from an ethic of finance, though not I think too far. But it is time to return explicitly to it.

3.   The root question from the past is this. Was the just price doctrine in the end right to accept the market system? And if so, should it have extended it to money?

To answer this, we need to divorce the market from the overarching philosophy of individualism with which it has usually been associated. I think that philosophy is false and un-Christian. It turns competitive relationships into an entire philosophy of basic human relationships, coupled with appeals for voluntary benevolence towards the deserving unfortunate. Socialists, including Christian Socialists, have usually gone further and dismissed the market itself on three grounds: 1. co-operation, not competition, is basic to human life; 2. profit is a dubious concept and production should be for use and not for profit; 3. the economic motive should be service, not self-interest. I have argued elsewhere[15] that these criticisms are either misplaced or do not bear the weight put upon them. Suffice it to say now that the political realm is prior to the economic, for without political order we should have anarchy, and that it is for the political order to set the basic framework of social justice. If that is done, the market is an excellent human device for getting a number of economic problems settled in a convenient, fair and efficient way, by an impersonal method less liable to abuse and to undue concentrations of power than any other.

There seems no reason why there should not be a market for money. Financial markets are not zero-sum games in which what one gains another loses. Properly run, they lead to general benefits in trading in goods and services, in trading in risks and liquidity, and in providing financial services. However, they are easily open to abuse by avarice. Classical economists tended to assume that markets were self-righting in the way that they thought separate elements in the economy, like one industry, were. But it is clear that they are not. Governments have to go much further than holding the ring. Moreover the same international dimension that makes the defence problems of national sovereign states so tricky operates in the financial market; this is more and more international when industrial, monetary, fiscal and wage-bargaining systems are national. We may well feel daunted at what needs to be striven for in both cases, but it has to be faced.

Underneath a market system there must be basic moral convictions which are explicitly taught, and punished if infringed. No collusion, no bribery, no cheating, respect for law. Because those who infringe can be economically weighty and politically powerful, strong agents of enforcement are needed. It will not do to leave enforcement to a kind of professional self-regulating code of ethics. Whatever may be said in criticism of professions, it is possible to do this with them to a considerable extent. But the world of business, banking and finance is not that of a profession. Its aim is to make a profit, and its legal responsibility is to its profit-seeking shareholders. We are paying the price of timidity in this sphere. The fact that markets are different means that they require different frameworks within which to operate. The markets for capital and labour are different from markets in most products. The capital market requires complex judgments, involving expertise which can easily get into the hands of a small élite, and investment decisions have big social repercussions. In the case of the labour market the possession of particular skills can make a worker very vulnerable, and a worker's life is crucially involved in market decisions.

What are the criteria which the Christian brings to the world of finance, industry and the social and political order? I have mentioned those of the Roman Catholic bishops of the USA. I myself have suggested four: 1. The basic equality of humans before God as more important than the things in which they are unequal. A universalism is implied here. Many secular humanists would agree with this, though they would find a different basis, perhaps in human rationality, or in 'nature'. 2. A concern for the poor and unprivileged; this stems from the ministry of Jesus and his attitude to *all* society's rejects. 3. From the Christian understanding of human dignity follows the desire that people should participate in decision-making in all matters which affect their well-being; and from the Christian understanding of human sinfulness follows the requirement that the exercise of power over others should be subject to check lest it be abused. 4. The state is an institution under God for the negative restraint of wrong doing and the positive furthering of conditions which favour rather than hinder the living of a good life.[16] Wogaman has listed five presumptions with which a Christian approaches moral judgments: 1. The goodness of created existence; 2. The value of individual life; 3. The unity of the human family in God; 4. The equality of all persons in God; 5. Human finiteness and sinfulness.[17]

There is a general similarity between these three examples, but this is not the occasion to examine them in detail. Our concern is with a method of bringing some such Christian presumptions alongside empirical investigations to arrive at a content in areas such as an ethic of finance which goes beyond generalizations. Before coming to some conclusions on this problem I turn aside to mention certain ethical problems in the general area of finance which need facing. I state them, I do not solve them. Indeed I do not think one person working on his or her own can solve them, nor that there is necessarily one solution. But to these matters I shall return at the end.

4. I mention five problems. It is clear that questions of finance quickly spill over into those of general economic and social policy such as production, saving, investment and inflation, but I shall try to avoid this as far as I can.

1. Taxation

As we know it, this is a relatively modern phenomenon. In feudal society the rulers' revenues came from personal estates, customary tributes, dues from vassals, tolls imposed on strangers and on traffic on roads and rivers, and booty from war, rapine and piracy. In times of special financial stringency there were subventions and donations which formally were voluntarily granted by the 'consent' of those paying them. Thus Aquinas treats taxation as an extraordinary act of a ruler and quite likely to be morally illicit; the presumption is that taxation is not a routine measure, and one legitimate only as a last resort and with the consent of the people.[18] Later casuistry held that taxation must accord with distributive justice, that is to say with ability to pay; this meant proportionate equality, together with a progressive scale of income and inheritance, but not at a confiscatory level, for that would infringe the rights of private property. The more lax casuistry held that it was not a strict moral duty to pay taxes, and perhaps not even sinful to evade them by deceit; the more rigorous casuistry condemned these views and said that there was an obligation to accept a penalty for not paying taxes, basing this on a theory of the state which stressed its task of pursuing the common good. The question was discussed under the heading of legal justice, though the term social justice has recently come to be used, particularly since the encyclical *Quadragesimo Anno* of 1931.

Luther's comments on taxation were characteristically unsystematic and inconsistent. In general he supported it on the biblical grounds of the authority of the state. He said that rulers could easily abuse their power to tax and that the revenue from taxation should be justly used, but in the end left the latter for the experts to resolve. Calvin held that taxation was necessary for rulers to maintain the disciplinary forces of the state, but that the church had the role under God of monitoring government policies. Protestant thinking on this theme was occasional and unsystematic, like Wesley's remark that a tax on horses would reduce the demand for oats and thus lower the price of it to the poor, and that the national debt should be halved, thus reducing the amount of interest on it and thus the need for taxes.

Later commentators in the heyday of *laisser-faire* tended to approve taxation on property to the extent of the benefits the government conferred on its owners, but no more. Beyond that private generosity should be relied on.

Today we tend to find the legacy of the scholastic tradition in debate with the legacy of the *laisser-faire* tradition. On the one hand progressive and proportionate taxes are advocated, especially because many of the poor are paying a bigger proportion of their income in taxes than the wealthy; on the other hand the contention is that taxes need to be reduced on the wealthier in order to avoid tax evasion and to ensure the efficient functioning of the economic system, when the benefits will trickle down through the whole economy to the poor. Here we come against the need for empirical evidence as to whether this really is so. Even supposing it is, there is the further question as to the balancing of efficiency against social justice, and of tax evasion against the extent of public control needed to deal with it.

A new issue which has emerged in recent decades is the claim by a few to be recognized as conscientious objectors to aspects of government policy, and not to pay a proportion of income tax which represents an equivalent proportion of government expenditure on it. It is one example of a demand for the recognition of selective conscientious objection, like those who are not pacifists in principle but want to object to particular wars which they may consider unjust. This is not an easy claim for states to allow. Their cohesion is threatened if citizens are allowed on any scale to be exempted from government requirements on the grounds of disagreement with particular government policies. I have received propaganda for refusing to pay water rates by those who object to the fluoridation of the water supply. I think we shall be forced to the conclusion that those who have strong views against aspects of public policy must be free to campaign to change them, and if they conscientiously think that they cannot co-operate with the state they must follow their conscientious judgment, but must be prepared to accept penalties in doing so.

2. Investment

Questions of public policy, the corporate responsibility of institutions like those controlling insurance and pension funds, and the decisions of the private investor, are interrelated. Keynes's demonstration that savings do not automatically spill over into productive investment, and that there are institutional obstacles to the economy being self-righting in this respect, has dominated controversies in economics ever since his *General Theory of Employment, Interest and Money* was published in 1936. It involved arguments on how far the government should positively promote investment and how far leave it to the unplanned operations of the market. Recent events have highlighted how much money changes hands on short-term considerations, and how far this produces inhuman effects. To what extent are the alleged advantages worth the harm done to human beings in achieving them? Moreover indiviual investors are slowly becoming more conscious of their wider responsibilities as shareholders, and also of the time and effort involved in trying to exercise them in large corporations. This awareness has gone a good deal further in the USA than in the UK, but pressure is growing here, through bodies like 'End Loans to South Africa', for ethical considerations to be brought to bear on investment policy in a scrutiny of portfolios. Some Unit Trusts specialize in ethical investments. Churches in particular are under some pressure from a significant portion of the membership of their representative bodies to scrutinize their investments.

This pressure has its place in arousing the public conscience and putting some of the commercial operations of some companies under critical scrutiny, but it is no substitute for government policies. Disinvestment by itself can merely lead to others less scrupulous picking up assets more cheaply.

Constitutionally different forms of industrial and commercial operation from the joint stock company could well be taken more seriously; all have both pros and cons. But as far as the joint company itself is concerned, the narrow legal view that it is the property of the shareholders and that the directors are solely responsible to them in terms of narrow criteria as to the good of the company is increasingly thought of as unsatisfactory, and a doubtful interpretation of the law.

3. Responsibility for the future

Economists tend to discount the future at a rate of 10% per annum, which means that they do not think much beyond fifteen years ahead. This is under half one generation. This is largely because of the uncertainties of forecasting. However, many issues demand a longer time-span. It is hard not to think that we have some responsibility for the situation that the 40% of the world's population who are children will have to face throughout their adult lives. This suggests the closing of as few options for the future as possible. It is a cautious and conservative attitude, and has to be balanced against others, such as the need to deal with manifest evils at the moment. Decision-making is rarely clear cut, with all considerations pointing one way; moral judgment is an art shown in the discrimination by which different considerations are weighed.

4. Aid and trade

Aid and trade policies from the relatively prosperous one-third world to the relatively poor two-thirds world cannot be left to the market forces generated by the prosperous. The discrepancy of power is too great. It makes it impossible for the two-thirds world to get out of its straitjacket. A free market left to itself tends to work in a 'to him that has shall be given' way, and further to increase the wealth and power of those who have already become wealthy and powerful. Of course aid must be given with wisdom, and of course Third World governments need themselves to follow wise policies; but beyond that we need more of the spirit behind the late mediaeval *montes pietatis* which deliberately operated in the interests of the poor, independently of the going rate on the market. How to get sufficient pressure on the one-third to induce it to behave in this way and adopt far-seeing trade policies is an unsolved problem; the two-thirds have not the power to compel it.

5. Control of the money supply

Governments have great power to arrange the framework of economic activity. Some people tremble at this, and especially at the injustice they can cause by varying the purchasing power of money, and by taking an easy route which leads to inflation instead of tackling underlying disequilibria. Inflation on a significant scale means that the powerful and unscrupulous individuals and groups flourish at the expense of the less powerful and those with integrity. Dempsey in his book on usury refers to 'institutional usury',[19] but this is not a very helpful phrase. Reacting against this, some want to put the creation of money entirely under an automatic mechanism, like the gold standard, in order to take such dangerous economic-political power away from governments, and compel countries to make the necessary adjustments as economic conditions change.

This runs to the opposite extreme, and subjects human beings to processes over which they have no say in a matter vital to their well-being. Social policies would be needed to help them to adjust, and those most keen on automatic mechanisms are usually least keen on such policies, preferring to rely on private benevolence to alleviate the misfortunes of others, except perhaps for the barest minimum of public provision, reminiscent of the 'less eligibility' days of the Victorian workhouse.

These are all complex issues which do not lend themselves to the simple right-and-wrong judgments which Christians often mistakenly seek. Tariffs were a good example. In the early years of this century when the Conservatives began to advocate tariffs, Christians who advocated *laisser-faire*, and who in England were identified with what was called the 'Nonconformist Conscience', campaigned against tariffs on the ground that they were immoral, and therefore un-Christian. It is dangerous to identify contingent judgments with heresy!

5.   How, then, can we approach such issues? We cannot move directly from the Bible, or a doctrine developed from the Bible (like the incarnation), or the concept of natural law, to a specific area of ethical decision, without intermediate steps, requiring empirical investigation, with all the hazards of uncertainty of evidence and of interpretation of evidence which that involves. We have to bring our Christian pre-suppositions (which to some extent will overlap with those of some secular humanists and those of other faiths) alongside the empirical data, allowing a reciprocal relationship to develop between the two, each throwing light on the other. This is best done in varying types of groups and consultations, drawing upon as wide a range as possible of relevant knowledge and experience. The history of Christian thinking on finance is a warning to avoid two errors. The first is to subsume human life under too fixed an interpretation of nature, and one which fuses the human, the animal and the inanimate too closely together. That was the mistake of the scholastics. The advocates of *laisser-faire* went even further along this road in treating the economic structure of the market as if its prescriptions were universal, akin to natural laws in the purely natural-science sense, like the laws of physics. The second error is to attach too much church authority to judgments made in changing situations, and thus to be inhibited from squarely looking at fresh evidence.

In weighing data Christians are quite likely to assess the weight and relevance of it differently. There can be disagreements about what are significant 'facts' and what are interpretations. The nearer one gets to specific policy recommendations, the more likely this is to be the case. Occasionally issues can be clear-cut. There can hardly be two Christian opinions on the legitimacy of liquidating Jews in gas chambers. But most areas of ethical decision are ambiguous. Thus if we can arrive at some broad consensus on the *direction* we want to go, a kind of middle ground, we will achieve a lot in helping Christians to form opinions, even if they end up in different camps on the best available policy for moving in the agreed direction. If we cannot get as far as that, owing to deep differences of opinion, we can at least put before those Christians who strongly advocate one line of policy the questions put to them by those who strongly advocate different ones. Listening to one another within the body of Christ is a salutary exercise, even if we have to go on living together with disagreements in ethics, as we do in doctrine.

Finance is an area which many feel is nearly as much out of control as is that of nuclear weapons. Avariciousness can easily have a field day and power be greatly abused.

Perhaps Christians spend too much time on sex issues, and maybe are in danger of doing so on questions of medical ethics, because they think that in these they may affect public policy, whereas on issues of nuclear and financial ethics they cannot. They may be too pessimistic. There are signs of this in the case of nuclear issues. But the area of finance remains a Cinderella. More attention might bring more results. We should not leave this area so largely neglected. Perhaps there is a third lesson to be learned, particularly by Protestants, from the unsatisfactory history of Christian thought on the ethics of finance: not to be so occasional and unsystematic, but to keep at it.

Appendix 2
Writings 1987–1991

A select list of books and articles up to the spring of 1981 was included in my *Explorations in Theology 9* and one from then until 1986 in my *The Future of Christian Ethics*; this list goes to the spring of 1991.

1987

The Future of Christian Ethics, SCM Press

'Is There a Christian Ethics of Finance?', Centre for Theology and Public Issues, Edinburgh University (reprinted with an amended title in Appendix 1 above)

Articles 'Community', 'Conflict', 'Sin', in *A Dictionary of Pastoral Care*, ed. Alastair V. Campbell, SPCK

'Theology and the Economy: The Roman Catholic Bishops in the USA', *Crucible*, July–September, pp. 98–107

1988

'Honest to God, The New Morality and Situation Ethics', in *God's Truth*, ed. Eric James, SCM Press, pp. 166–76

'Convergence and Divergence in Social Theology: The Roman Catholic Church and the World Council of Churches', *The Ecumenical Review*, Vol. 40.2, pp. 194–203

'Christian Faith and Capitalism', a review article of Ulrich Duchrow's *Global Economy*, ibid., pp. 279–86

'Fifty Years from the Oxford Conference', *Crucible*, January–March, pp. 2–10

'Christian Socialism Becalmed', *Theology*, Vol. 91, no. 739, pp. 24–32

1989

'Twenty Years after *Populorum Progressio*: an Appraisal of Pope John Paul's Commemorative Encyclical', *Theology* Vol. 92, no. 750, pp. 519–25

'Humanity, Nature and the Integrity of Creation', *The Ecumenical Review*, Vol. 41.4, pp. 552–63

'Reflections on Love, Power and Justice', in *The Nuclear Weapons Debate: Theological and Ethical Issues*, ed. Richard J. Bauckham and R. John Elford, SCM Press, pp. 115–30

1990

'Comment on Duchrow's paper "Politics and Economic Wellbeing and Justice: A Global View"', in *Studies in Christian Ethics*, Vol. 3.1, pp. 93–99

'The Justice Model and Forgiveness', in *Justice, Guilt and Forgiveness*, Centre for Theology and Public Issues, Edinburgh University

Review of Donald A. Hay, *Economics Today: A Christian Critique*, *The Journal of Theological Studies*, New series, Vol. 41.2, pp. 792–800

1991

'Christian Ethics', in *A Companion to Ethics*, ed. Peter Singer, Blackwell, pp. 91–105

Notes

1. An Overview

1. Major Douglas died in 1952. Another leading churchman who adopted his ideas for a time was Dr Hewlett Johnson, who had also trained as an engineer. Later he became known as the 'Red' Dean of Canterbury because of his enthusiasm for Soviet Russia. An account of the influence of the Christendom group can be found in John Oliver, *The Church and the Social Order: Social Thought in the Church of England 1918–39*, 1968; and its influence is seen in Philip Mairet, *The National Church and the Social Order*, Church Information Board, 1957. What led the writers I have mentioned to such blind self-confidence in their writings on economics is not entirely clear, and is beyond the scope of this book. It was probably a rigid understanding of natural law, from the precepts of which, as they understood it, the framework of an economic order could be deduced. This ruled out the possibility of economics as an independent discipline. Marxism may also have had an influence, and some fringe writers on economics like J.A. Hobson, who were wrestling with the problems of booms and slumps, about which economists seemed sanguine. There are still a few old-style advocates of Social Credit in Britain. In Canada the Social Credit party was dominant in Alberta from 1935 to 1971, and in British Columbia from 1952–58, 1962–72, and it is still powerful. It was also represented in the Ottawa Parliament from 1935 to 1980, when it lost its six seats. However, Douglas's ideas were abandoned in the 1930s for right-wing agrarian policies, and employee participation in profit-sharing. In any case the Central Bank of Canada would have prevented runaway inflation; by 1942 nine of Alberta's laws were disallowed. There have also been one or two Social Credit MPs in New Zealand. Social Credit is examined by Hugh Gaitskell in *What Everybody wants to know about Money*, ed. G.D.H. Cole, 1933.

2. One of the activities in the working-class parish in which I first served after ordination, St John, Park, Sheffield, had been a Monday evening Savings Club. The result was that members of the congregation tended to use their money more far-sightedly than others and 'bettered' themselves, moving out to more salubrious areas of Sheffield, from where they would return to church on a Sunday evening in the summer. The 1939–45 war broke up this habit. A more corporate and recent example of the same concern is church encouragement of Credit Unions.

3. Almsgiving (including bequests) was often practised (and advocated) as a remedy for sins. Other theologians taught that what was surplus to keeping one in one's station in life was due to the poor as a matter of justice, not charity. St

Paul is clear that almsgiving should be a cheerful response to God's graciousness already experienced (I Cor. 9.7).

4. A brief treatment, with references, can be found in my Scott Holland lectures, *Church and Society in the Late Twentieth Century: The Economic and Political Task*, 1983, Ch. 2.

5. For Christian Socialism see my *Church and Society* (n. 4), Ch. 1, and Edward Norman, *The Victorian Christian Socialists*, 1987.

6. E.g. *Quadragesimo Anno* (1931), *Mater et Magistra* (1961), *Populorum Progressio* (1967), *Octogesima Adveniens* (1971), *Laborem Exercens* (1981), *Sollicitudo Rei Socialis* (1988), *Centesimus Annus* (1991), see Ch. 6 n. 22.

7. See note 5 above.

8. Cf. M.B. Reckitt, *Maurice to Temple*, 1948.

9. Cf. Walter Rauschenbusch, *A Theology for the Social Gospel*, Macmillan, New York 1918, and three of the earlier books of Reinhold Niebuhr: *Moral Man and Immoral Society*, Scribner 1932 (SCM Press 1963); *An Interpretation of Christian Ethics*, Harper 1935 (SCM Press 1936); and *Beyond Tragedy*, Harper 1937 (Nisbet 1938).

10. There were seven volumes connected with the Oxford Conference, the most relevant to this book being W.A. Visser 't Hooft and J.H. Oldham, *The Church and its Function in Society*, and *The Christian Faith and the Common Life*, with an introduction by J.H. Oldham, 1938.

11. Of the four volumes of essays connected with the Geneva Conference those most relevant to this book are *Economic Growth in World Perspective*, ed. Denys Munby, and *Christian Social Ethics in a Changing World*, ed. John C. Bennett, 1966.

12. The best-known contemporary exponent of Neo-Calvinist economic thought is Bob Goudzwaard, especially in his book *Capitalism and Progress: a Diagnosis of Western Society*, (ET Eerdmans, Grand Rapids, Michigan 1979). Some of its proposals are 'liberal' and 'progressive'. There is a brief account of it in my *Church and Society* (n. 4), Ch. 4.; see also *Reformed Faith and Economics*, ed. R.L. Stivers, University Press of America, Lanham, Maryland 1989.

13. Cf. my *Church and Society* (n. 4), Ch. 3.

14. Both quoted in Aart van der Berg, *Churches Speak Out on Economic Issues: A Survey of Several Church Statements*, World Council of Churches, Commission on the Churches' Participation in Development, Geneva 1990, pp. 67f.

2. Understanding Economics and Its Limits

1. Saving and investment are not the same thing. It is possible to set aside resources for the future and do nothing with them (e.g. keep them in a stocking), or to invest them productively. One of J.M. Keynes's contributions was to stress the importance of this distinction.

2. Jevons of Manchester University made a major mistake in expecting British coal reserves to be exhausted rapidly. *The Limits to Growth* extrapolations of the Club of Rome in 1972 are a recent example of the same mistake, taken up by some ecologists. Imaginative writers sometimes like to picture a world of such abundance that economic choices no longer have to be made, but this improbable vision can be banished from our present problems of choice.

3. For Social Credit see Chapter 1, n. 1; there is still a small Social Credit group in Britain.

4. J.M. Keynes, 'Economic Possibilities for our Grandchildren', in *Essays in Persuasion*, Collected Works, Vol. 9.

5. Denys Munby, *Christianity and Economic Problems*, 1956, pp. 44f.

6. Gary Becker, *The Economic Approach to Human Affairs*, Chicago 1972.

7. The Italian economist V. Pareto elaborated on 'optimum' economic states where it would be impossible to make anyone better off without making someone else worse off. This is not a different value, but assumes the supreme value of efficiency in the economic sense. Note how different this can be from efficiency in an engineering sense; a mechanism might be highly efficient in engineering terms but inefficient in economic terms.

8. F.A. von Hayek, in several books, especially his trilogy *Law, Legislation and Liberty*, of which the second volume is entitled *The Mirage of Social Justice*, 1976, argues this.

9. They have been called the divine orders of creation. The best treatment is still Emil Brunner's *The Divine Imperative*, ET 1937. Other theologians have used other names for the same concept, e.g. Bonhoeffer's 'mandates'. Brunner points out that there is a fourth and all-pervasive divine order, that of culture. It is possible to develop an ecclesiology which regards the Christian church as an order of creation, but sociologically considered it is not.

10. J.M. Buchanan of George Mason University, Washington, won a Nobel Prize for economics in 1986 for his contribution to it.

11. All public policies involve trade-offs: e.g., will redistribution destroy incentives? How far do the wealthy need the inducement of a lot more money, and the poor a threat to reduce what money they have, to make them work?

12. France learned that in 1981, when an attempt to go it alone had to be reversed. 1990 was the eighth year of growth of the world economy, but it looked like running into a recession, defined as two or more quarters of negative growth. A trade war, debt defaults, or oil-price rises could easily provoke one. The central banks co-operated in October 1987 to avert a crisis. Up to a point recessions are made less traumatic in welfare states where expenditure on social security rises. Public spending in the Organization for Economic Co-operation and Development rose from 28% of gross national product in 1960 to 41% in 1989, and it does not shrink so fast as private spending in a recession. A shift from manufacture to personal services also helps, because they are less sensitive to changes in demand, less capital-intensive, and they cannot be put aside and stored.

13. The reality of unemployment is more complex. There is reason to suppose that the long-term unemployed hardly affect wage rates, and that they could be paid to work without inflationary consequences. So there is now talk of a NAIRU, or non-accelerating inflationary rate of unemployment.

14. M0 and M3 are different ways of measuring money in circulation, according to what is included, but it is not necessary to delve into this for our present purpose.

3. The Response of Christian Social Theory to the Rise of Capitalism

1. Since the appendix was written, as a lecture given in Edinburgh University in 1978, a defence of the traditional position has been advanced by Michael Schluter of the Jubilee Centre in Cambridge, *The Old Testament Ban on Usury*. The Jubilee Centre is an evangelical Anglican research body which produces informed work on current social issues, such as aging and the carers of the aged, and personal debt crises. It relates its work closely to biblical texts. Schluter argues that Old Testament laws are still binding unless there is a specific command in the New Testament to abrogate them, such as Mark 7.19 (which says Jesus made all meats clean), and Col. 2.16 (which refers dismissively to meat, drink, sabbath and new moon). He holds that Matt. 25.25ff. (the parable of the talents) does not abrogate the ban on usury and that Calvin's relaxation of the ban on usury was a mistake (*Harmony of the Four Last Books of the Pentateuch*, vol. 3, p. 132); he thought of usury solely as an individual and personal matter and not one of general social relationships. I shall refer to this use of the Bible in Chapter 7. Schluter also thinks that he can make a general case against interest to the non-Christian public on the grounds that it breaks down the extended family and the local community by encouraging mobility, and that it undermines national solidarity and identity. This archaism was characteristic of traditional social theology, and of the Christendom group (discussed with reference to Social Credit in Chapter 1), and is also characteristic of a Christian retreat to the local level which is expressed in some ecumenical literature (see Chapter 6). Schluter dislikes big companies because their power relationships are bad. So they may be. But the small factory employers in industrial Britain in the last century were notoriously bad in their power relationships. At any scale the use of power has to be kept under scrutiny.

2. The theme was followed up in 1949 with a book by V.A. Demant, *Religion and the Decline of Capitalism*, and in 1977 with a further one by me, *Religion and the Persistence of Capitalism* (1979). The present book is in a sense a fourth in the sequence. It might have been called *Religion and the Triumph of Capitalism*? The question mark, however, would have been necessary. See the Preface to this book and Chapter 5.

3. Tawney (1929, p. 189) had two other criticisms, less well focussed. The first is that Christianity became privatized and a sharp gulf was created between personal and social morality. One can see what he means; there is much spurious private, individualistic piety about in Protestantism, and to a lesser extent in Catholicism: in particular a common interpretation of the Lutheran doctrine of the two realms has been criticized as making too sharp a division between the public and personal realms. Nevertheless there is a difference between the two, most dramatically discussed in Reinhold Niebuhr's *Moral Man and Immoral Society*, Harper 1932 (SCM Press 1963). Tawney's second criticism is that the church ceased to *enforce* any social obligations on its members; it was content with urging private benevolence. This raises many questions, especially how far it presupposes a Christendom situation which has now passed. In a pluralistic society only a sect can try to enforce such disciplines. Further, the history of the area where churches and

sects both do attempt to enforce disciplines, sexual ethics, shows the many hazards involved.

4. The positive influence of Protestantism on the rise of capitalism has been much discussed since Max Weber's essays on the subject, especially *The Protestant Ethic and the Spirit of Capitalism*, ET by Talcott Parsons 1930. This is sometimes called the Weber-Tawney thesis. Some have written as if it held that Protestantism was a main factor in the rise of capitalism. In fact the thesis was a very modest one: that there were elements in Calvinist theology which in the century after Calvin had an affinity with the spirit of diligence, thrift and enterprise that capitalism required. This seems clearly to have been the case, and to have had a discernible but now nearly faded influence in several countries, Britain being one. But many other factors were at work, and capitalism has triumphed in non-Christian cultures. For an example see S. Gordon Redding, *The Spirit of Chinese Capitalism*, 1990, which focusses on the forty million Chinese of South-East Asia and their entrepreneurial culture; its base appears to a family structure of filial piety, a work ethic – and a cult of divination!

5. Cf. *Butler's Fifteen Sermons*, ed. T.A. Roberts 1970, and C.D. Broad, *Five Types of Ethical Theory*, 1930.

6. Investigations into the influence of clergy and ministers on the development of economics are being carried on by Professor Salim Rashid of the University of Illinois and Professor A.M.C. Waterman of the University of Manitoba, cf. the references in Chapter 6 (n. 20) and in my *Church and Society in the Late Twentieth Century*, 1983, pp. 165, 166 and 173. Waterman has produced a major study of Malthus, *Revolution, Economics and Religion: Christian Political Economy 1798–1833*, 1991.

7. Cf. the references to Christian Socialism in Chapter 1.

8. The Oxford Chair was founded in 1825; the second one was at the new University College, London, in 1827.

9. Cf. Charles Booth, *Life and Labour of the People in London* (17 vols.), 1889–92.

10. Cf. H. Thomas and C. Logan, *Mondragon: An Economic Analysis*, 1981.

11. The distribution of surplus benefits beyond whatever minimal level is established raises further problems to which there is no simple answer. The usual criteria suggested are need, merit and legal right. In practice policy is unlikely to follow any one of them exclusively, but to arrive at some mixture of the three. Christian theology has not suggested a fourth one nor ruled out any of the three. Its stress would be on the first, then on the third (because of the importance of stability in the social order if ongoing human purposes are to be achieved without the unpredictable end product of disorder), and lastly on the second, which it would handle cautiously.

12. John-Paul II makes these points strongly in his two social encyclicals *Laborem Exercens* (1981) and *Sollicitudo Rei Socialis* (1988); this amounts to a condemnation of *laisser-faire* capitalism, but the theme is not explicitly and closely pursued, so that the points have been read, e.g. by M. Novak, in other ways (see Chapter 6 n. 1).

13. Cf. 'Church, Community and State in Relation to the Economic Order',

in *The Churches Survey Their Task*, introduction by J.H. Oldham, Report of the Oxford Conference of 1937.

14. *Facing the Future as Christians and Socialists*, ed. David Ormrod, Christian Socialist Movement 1985. The aims of the CSM range more widely into Christian unity, world peace and disarmament; in terms of the organization of an economic order it refers in a general way to redistribution of wealth; the key phrase is 'the common ownership and democratic control of the productive resources of the earth'.

15. A classic statement is Michael Young, *The Rise of the Meritocracy 1870–2033, An Essay on Education and Equality*, 1962. His point is that the old élite was so indefensible that it could never feel sure of the legitimacy of its power and wealth; whereas a meritocracy would be worse because it would feel confident of its legitimacy. The result would be neglect of the fostering of the contribution of the less intelligent to society.

4. The Marxist Response to the Rise of Capitalism

1. This is the theme of Lenin's *Imperialism: The Highest Stage of Capitalism*, 1913.

2. K. Marx, *Collected Works*, 1976, Vol. 5, p. 47.

3. Modern economics with its marginal analysis had not developed when *Das Kapital* began to be published (cf. Ch. 2). For an account of the problems of the Soviet economic system as it was before the days of *perestroika* see A. Nove, *The Economics of Feasible Socialism*, 1983, and M. Desai, *Marxist Economics*, 1979.

4. Cf. Lenin, *The State and Revolution*, 1917.

5. K. Marx, *Preface to a Contribution to a Critique of Political Economy*, 1854. There is some uncertainty in Marx at this point, which has been the source of divergent interpretations ever since. In the third of his *Theses on Feuerbach*, 1845, he says that men can change their circumstances. There is also uncertainty on the relation of base and superstructure in *The German Ideology*, 1846. Professor David McClellan is the most thorough and accessible of the interpreters of Marxism; two of his many books are *The Thought of Karl Marx*, 1971, and *Marxism after Marx*, 1979. Of the many discussions of Christianity and Marxism, Nicholas Lash, *A Matter of Hope*, 1981, may be singled out.

6. Karl Mannheim, *Ideology and Utopia*, 1936, remains a classic study in the sociology of knowledge, despite the great amount of writing since. The Frankfurt Institute of Social Research, founded in 1923 and exiled to the United States through the 1939–45 war, came to terms with the rise in the standard of living of the working class, but despaired of that class as now being consumption-orientated and led astray in this by the media; their hope was in an *avant garde* of aesthetically-minded intellectuals. Mannheim in his own way also falls back on intellectuals; this has happened many times among 'progressive' thinkers. The Frankfurt School in the shape of Max Horkheimer, Theodor Adorno and Jürgen Habermas placed great stress on Marx's early writings.

7. Dimitrov in the dock at the Leipzig fire trial.

8. G.V. Plekhanov, Preface to *The ABC of Communism*, 1923, who was the first to use the term 'dialectical materialism'.

9. There is an interesting discussion in Alistair Kee's *Marx and the Failure of Liberation Theology*, 1990, on Marxism as a phenomenon, and its relation to religion in particular. He thinks the liberation theologians are not Marxist enough in not accepting Marx's criticism of the dimension of the supernatural and transcendent in religion and holding that all human knowledge is only of the human. This is contrary to what I am saying. Many other modern thinkers besides Marx, of course, take this position.

10. Clodovis Boff, *Theology and Praxis: Epistemological Foundations*, Maryknoll 1976.

11. Structural functional sociology, particularly associated with the name of Talcott Parsons, analyses societies as self-equilibrating systems, which clearly explains stability. Marxist sociology is concerned with dynamic social change.

12. *Instructions on Certain Aspects of the Theology of Liberation*, 1982, and *Instructions on Christian Freedom and Liberation*, 1984, both from the Sacred Congregation for the Doctrine of the Faith.

13. Cf. the second edition of G. Gutiérrez, *A Theology of Liberation* (still the best introduction), which modifies his previous reliance on the dependency theory, that world capitalism extracts surplus value to the detriment of Latin America; he also substitutes class conflict for class struggle.

14. A convenient survey to 1984, when it was first published, is Theo Witvliet, *A Place in the Sun: An Introduction to Liberation Theology in the Third World*.

15. Cf. Paulo Freire, *Pedagogy of the Oppressed*, 1970.

16. An anonymous writer said of Marx that 'he was the most successful ideologist of the modern era; that is, a prophet who, by including romantic sensibility with industrial statistics, dressed myth in the clothing of science, and offered thereby a secularized mankind the most plausible travesty that it had a sure means of a perfect and permanent end of its psychic pains and its material wants and could thus achieve full realization of its essence in a state of total freedom and total supposed felicity' (*The Economist*, 8 December 1975).

17. R.R. Ruether, 'Ecology and Human Liberation: A Conflict Between the Theology of History and the Theology of Nature?', in *To Change the World: Christology and Culture Criticism*, 1981.

18. Ernst Bloch's *Principle of Hope*, ET 1986, is an instance of a Marxist author who has influenced several Western European theologians, particularly Jürgen Moltmann; see especially the latter's *Theology of Hope*, ET 1967, and many subsequent books. He moves from the important point that churches should be a constant source of eschatological unrest in society (which they find much harder than their conserving role), to maintaining 1. that those who hope for fulfilment beyond this life resign themselves to supporting the *status quo*, though there is ample evidence that this does not necessarily follow; 2. that truth lies in the future and proves itself by moving the world towards its future transformation, which will be radically new and not a fulfilment of the present. Nevertheless we are to activate present possibilities which lead in the direction of this radically new future. How we are to do this, since we cannot know what will be radically new, is obscure.

19. There have been other non-Marxist theories of the growing problems of

free-market capitalism. In *Capitalism, Socialism and Democracy*, 1942, Joseph Schumpeter argued that, because of the 'creative destruction' that capitalism causes, its internal dynamics have become so risky that only monopolies can face them, and entrepreneurs will become obsolescent. It hardly seems so. Fred Hirsch, in *The Social Limits to Growth*, 1977, was really writing of the social limits to private consumption: the incentives to work in order to obtain 'positional goods', whose enjoyment depends on their scarcity, will prove less effective as they become more widely spread and their enjoyment is diminished. The more suburbia spreads, the less desirable it becomes; greater car ownership jams the roads; bigger crowds at beauty-spots ruin them. If everyone stands on tip-toe no one sees any better. Hirsch was also concerned with the lack in a market philosophy of the fostering of a moral base (which was a concern of Demant and others). Then there are the various claims about the ecological future of the world made by the Green movement, with its varied manifestations. To the extent that they are well founded they apply to the whole globe, not just to capitalist societies. Indeed Soviet-style economies are among the worst offenders.

5. *The Triumph of Capitalism?*

1. It also leaves out efficiency in the economic sense, because it assumes that the problem of production has been solved in pre-communist society, so that the abundance created will have made communism possible.

2. Centralized power has been a particular danger to African states newly independent from colonial rule. Partly it has been due to the effort to overcome tribalism (since rival political parties have tended to be tribally based), but also it is because pre-colonial Africa was collectivist and so perhaps had roots which were naturally socialist in the centralized sense. Europe had to change radically to cope with the dynamics of agricultural and industrial change, and is still trying to find the right balance between the personal and the corporate. African states may also have to face a radical change. The Xhosa have a proverb, 'people are people through other people', an insight which needs preserving amid radical change.

3. The term comes from C.B. Macpherson, *The Political Theory of Possessive Individualism*, 1962.

4. There are good treatments of the significance of the person in John Macmurray's Gifford Lectures of 1953 and 1954, *The Form of the Personal*: Vol. 1, *The Self as Agent*, 1957; Vol. 2, *Persons in Relation*, 1961; also in the neo-Thomist Jacques Maritain's *True Humanism*, ET 1938, and *The Person and the Common Good*, 1947. Both have been unduly neglected recently.

5. 'Think tanks' like the Institute of Economic Affairs, the Adam Smith Institute, and the Centre for Policy Studies, all in the United Kingdom, hardly admit this, and continue to publish studies on privatization and other topics which ignore it. The only parallel on the Left is the latest, the Institute of Public Policy Research.

6. See the seventh annual report (1990) on British Social Attitudes published by Social and Community Planning Research, an independent non-profit body.

7. Oscar Lange, *The Economics of Socialism*, ed. A. Nove and D.M. Null, 1972.

8. Abel Aganbegyan, *The Challenge: Economics of Perestroika*, 1988.

9. See M.P. Fogarty, *Christian Democracy in Western Europe*, 1957.

10. See n. 4 above.

11. See F.A. von Hayek, *The Fatal Conceit: The Errors of Socialism*, 1988. Once more he stresses the market as a discovery process whereby people unknown to one another co-ordinate their actions in a process too diverse and complicated for any government to plan. He applies the same idea to moral values. No one mind can grasp the full implications of a moral order and provide arguments which can justify it. But some moral rules involving promise-keeping and fairness, and some moral practices involving legal justice, property rights and the rule of law have been responsible for the survival of the vast majority of the human race, so it is wise to take them seriously. Hostility to the market arises because people confuse small face-to-face groups with the morality of the large world of strangers.

12. The exception is the long-term unemployed who no longer affect the labour market and could be engaged in socially and economically useful activities, for instance in the construction industry which still uses much unskilled labour, without risking inflation (cf. Chapter 2, n. 3).

13. Modern industry is vastly more productive with a smaller work-force and that more skilled. Unskilled jobs are fast fading. The less technically skilled in aptitude all have personal qualities which should be used in the many personal services needed in a modern, largely urban, industrialized society, in which people tend to live much longer. Society should be prepared to use the wealth produced by the greater productivity to pay for this rather than for increased private consumption. The whole area of 'care in the community', now in the doldrums through lack of public resources devoted to it, would be transformed if this was done. Only a small number are unemployable and they, of course, need sensitive care.

14. Taxes have been 56% of gross domestic product. Trade union membership has been 90% of blue collar and 80% of white collar workers. The average wage differential between skilled and unskilled labour became as low as 25% in the 1980s.

15. Cf. Hayek, n. 11 above.

16. See *Market Socialism*, ed. Julian le Grand and Saul Estrin, 1989, where many suggestions are made.

17. Different structures include: 1. ESOPs (Employee Share Ownership Plans), where workers have a stake in the undertaking, beyond just profit-sharing. Mrs Thatcher favoured this. 2. Partnership Companies, where the workers own more than 50% of the share capital: the National Freight Consortium is an example. 3. Worker Co-operatives, like the John Lewis partnership in the retail trade, or Mondragon in Spain. They need competent managers. They can be hard to start (or to shut down), and slow to adjust to market changes, but are strongly participatory and egalitarian in tendency. 4. Consumers' Co-operatives.

6. The Economic Order in Recent Christian Thought

1. The nearest approach is perhaps the laymen's rival report to the Commission of the Roman Catholic bishops of the USA on the economy, *The Lay Commission on Catholic Social Teaching and the US Economy*, 1986. It is discussed at the end of this chapter. A similar point of view was expressed two years earlier in Michael Novak's *The Spirit of Democratic Capitalism*, New York 1984. A British counterpart was the essays edited by Digby Anderson, *The Kindness that Kills*, 1984.

2. It has also affected Roman Catholic thought to some extent (see n. 1), but there are stronger correctives to it in its tradition of moral and social theology which was never lost, even if it was somewhat submerged and distorted during the dramatic growth of industrialism.

3. It originally appeared in *Women's Own*, October 1987, and is quoted in full by Brian Griffiths in *Christianity and Conservatism*, ed. Michael Alison and David Edwards, 1990.

4. Most of the more extreme New Right do not go quite as far as this, and not so far as their nineteenth-century predecessors with their support of the workhouse as the last refuge of the indigent. They mostly advocate provision of a minimum standard of living for a citizen, and one which is sufficiently severe to induce those receiving it to stir themselves to escape from it, which it is assumed that most, but not all, of them can if they have the will to do so.

5. See n. 3 above. Note also his books *Morality in the Market Place*, 1982, and *The Creation of Wealth*, 1984.

6. Catherine Mulholland (ed.), *Ecumenical Reflections on Political Economy*, World Council of Churches, Geneva 1988.

7. *Our Common Future: World Commission on Environment and Development*, 1987; it advocates 'sustainable development'.

8. The result of a joint meeting of CCPD and the Lutheran World Federation at Sao Paulo in Brazil, 1987.

9. This shows a naive faith in the moral purity of trade unions, rather like the Marxist view of workers as the innocent class because it has no one below it to exploit. To take one example from the United Kingdom, the printing unions had a stranglehold on the newspaper industry for years, treating it as a private fief. In the end this drove the entire Fleet Street section of the industry away from its centre there in London, but it took an even more ruthless and financially powerful Press baron, Rupert Murdoch, to break the union hold. It was a sad tale on all sides.

10. I have reviewed Duchrow's book *Global Economy: A Confessional Issue for the Church?*, 1987, in some detail in *The Ecumenical Review*, October 1989. It is published for CCPD by the World Council of Churches. In 1990 CCPD published *The Political Economy of the Holy Spirit*, the writing up of two group meetings of twelve people by Julia de Santa Ana, Konrad Reiser and Ulrich Duchrow. It sets up an easy target (but necessary as far as it goes) in attacking the 'mystique' of the market, and produces a sustained and rhetorical condemnation of its 'insidious' power, without precisely examining its economic function. At one point it says its aim is not to reject the market but to regulate it in such a way that neither injustice nor marginalization occurs (p. 24); but the

promise to return to this point is not fulfilled. Instead there is a major attack on the role of instrumental reason in the modern world, on institutions, and on bureaucracies. It is said that the poor and oppressed do not live by instrumental reason. Most of this is an evasion not only of basic economic problems but also of basic political problems of government. The context of the booklet suggests that consultation has been abandoned in favour of advocacy by a like-minded group. Theologically it suggests a throw back to the more simple forms of the Social Gospel outlook, according to which by following the love ethic of Jesus societies entirely free of power struggles and competition can be created.

11. It is worth noting that all theological statements can be distorted in use. The Barmen Declaration can be interpreted pietistically, the doctrine of election nationalistically (as by the Boers), and the Orders of Creation were exploited by the 'German Christians' under Hitler, who added race to them.

12. 1. *Economics To-day: A Christian Critique*, 1989. Hay is a Fellow of Jesus College, Oxford. I have reviewed his book in detail in the *Journal of Theological Studies*, October 1990; 2. *God the Economist: The Doctrine of God and the Political Economy*, Fortress Press 1989. Meeks is Professor of Systematic Theology and Philosophy at Eden Theological Seminary.

13. It is the more unfortunate because in one place he does refer to choice (p. 53) and in one to marginal utility (p. 161), but in both cases passes quickly on in a way which shows that he has not appreciated their significance; for instance, he moves at once from marginal utility to insatiable needs (probably meaning wants). Although from the notes and bibliography it is clear that he has read widely around the penumbra of economics, there is little in them by what we might call technical economists. Another book on these issues by a theologian is J. Philip Wogaman, *Economics and Ethics: A Christian Enquiry*, 1986. It is well argued.

14. See Chapter 3.

15. See Chapter 1.

16. See Chapter 2.

17. This will run into the charge of 'speciesism', a term we owe to Professor Peter Singer of Monash University, Melbourne. It is a charge of arrogance on the part of humans for exalting themselves over other species. It can, and must, be met. Some Christians are taking it too seriously. For example the work of the Holy Spirit in creation is used to minimize the distinction between humans and other species; St Paul in I and II Corinthians repeatedly stresses persons as temples of the Holy Spirit.

18. CCPD has published a useful book, A. van den Berg, *Churches Speak out on Economic Issues*, WCC 1990. It does not deal with the Roman Catholic Church, but collects statements from other churches, noting how difficult it is to find any from the Orthodox or from the global South; the churches which speak out are mostly from the 'same middle class and upper class writing élite' of the North. There is an assessment of their merits and deficiencies.

19. Recognized officially for the first time in the Declaration on Religious Liberty of the Second Vatican Council.

20. The story of papal teaching on private property is interesting. Primarily it goes back to Aquinas, who argued that it is expedient because people look

after what is their own in a way they do not what is common, i.e. they are sinful. (It follows that property should be widely distributed; indeed all should possess it.) Later Locke was to argue for it on the grounds that what God (or nature) has provided in common could be privately appropriated if one had 'mixed one's labour' with it, so long as 1. enough is left for others; 2. no more is taken than can be made use of before it spoils; 3. no more is taken than a man can work on by his own labour. Papal social teaching from 1891 was strongly anti-socialist because of the supposed inviolability of private property, bringing in arguments stemming from Locke as well as from Aquinas. This is an argument from human dignity more than human sin. *Mater et Magistra* (1961) adds two more: that private property safeguards political freedom, and is sanctioned by the gospel. *Gaudium et Spes* (1965) abandoned the Locke element, and it is absent from the encyclicals of John-Paul II. The tendency now is to soften the stress on the sanctity of private property and to relativize the right to it, especially if one has more than one needs and others lack necessities (*Populorum Progressio* 1967). This is a return to a position widely held by the fathers of the early church in what is known as the patristic period. Further, the hostility to 'socialism', so marked in *Rerum Novarum*, has been replaced in John-Paul II by a stress on the priority of labour. However, an analysis of the market is still missing from Roman Catholic social theology. Cf. A.M.C. Waterman, 'The Intellectual Context of *Rerum Novarum*', in *Review of Social Economy*, November 1991.

21. The Sacred Congregation for the Defence of the Faith gave two cautionary, but not entirely hostile, Instructions on Liberation Theology in 1984 and 1986 (cf. Ch. 4, n. 12).

22. In May 1991 Pope John Paul II issued his third social encyclical, *Centesimus Annus*, to commemorate the centenary of *Rerum Novarum*. By then this book had gone to press, so that it is possible only to add this very brief comment. The later part of the encyclical is influenced by the events in Eastern Europe since 1989, as this book has been, and its reactions are broadly similar. The Pope says that these events do not mean the unambiguous triumph of capitalism, either institutionally or as an individualistic ideology. The free market is an efficient economic instrument, but it needs strong appropriate controls if the basic needs of the whole of society are to be met. Personal self-interest must be brought into harmony with the interests of society. (The stress on the priority of labour in the Pope's first two social encyclicals is not found here.) The church's social teaching has no one model of society to propose, but offers 'an orientation toward the common good'. Here the Pope calls for the developed countries to get away from giving out of their surplus to a sacrifice of income and power, and for changes in life-styles, in models of production and consumption, and in established structures. No illustrations are given of what this might mean. Meanwhile the Third World must not isolate itself from, nor be shut out of, international trade.

The earlier part of the encyclical is hampered by the compliments paid to *Rerum Novarum*. In 1891 the Roman Catholic church was still reacting as if in a beleaguered fortress to the Enlightenment, the French Revolution and the Industrial Revolution. It identified socialism with atheistic rationalism and totalitarianism. An excessive stress on the continuity of church teaching prevents the new encyclical from breaking free from this in its comments on *Rerum Novarum*. We can also recall that in 1851 Pius IX, who had fled from his Papal State in 1848 and was restored under the protection of French troops in 1850, issued an encyclical *Nostis et Nobiscum* in the course of which he said that workers must not be deluded by Socialism or Communism, and must obey the state (quoting Rom. 13.1–7). Social encyclicals also suffer, and this latest one is no exception, by a complacency which avoids any criticism of church teaching and practice.

Following the example of John XXIII the encyclical is addressed not only to Christians but 'to all men and women of good will', but the implications of this are not followed through in the text. Its general stance is indicated by the remark that there can be no genuine solution of the social question apart from the gospel.

23. *Economic Justice for All: Catholic Social Teaching and the US Economy*, 1986. (The Canadian bishops' conference had made a similar but less extended study in 1983. For the Laymen's Report see n. 1 above.) In their first draft the bishops set a target of 3–4% unemployment, but they removed a precise figure from later texts. The lack of an analysis of the economic system of the USA is indicated in two other ways. 1. They do not distinguish three causes of unemployment: frictional (changing jobs), structural (long-term changes in demand) and cyclical (the booms and slumps of the Trade Cycle). 2. They implicitly accept a 'Keynesian' analysis of how the economy adjusts or fails to adjust, as against e.g. a monetarist one. *If* this amount of detail (beyond a middle level) is to be gone into, these different analyses have to be evaluated, and not one of them assumed. This brings us back again to the role of expertise in the background to ethical decision-making. See also *Prophetic Visions and Economic Realities: Protestants and Jews and Catholics Confront the Bishops' Letter on the Economy*, ed. Charles R. Strain, 1989.

7. The Bible, Doctrine and Economic Issues

1. Cf. Richard Hooker, *Treatise on the Laws of Ecclesiastical Policy*, especially Book 5 (1597). There is an Everyman edition.

2. The word is *homoousios*, which first appeared in the credal statement of the Council of Nicea (325), and remains in what is called the Nicene Creed in the phrase 'of one substance (or Being) with the Father' (referring to Jesus Christ). It is almost universally accepted by trinitarian Christians.

3. The ordination of women to the priesthood and episcopate is resolving itself into an argument about the fixity of tradition (with the exception of biblical literalists).

4. Before historical-critical methods developed, the church took refuge in allegory in dealing with contradictions and anomalies; critical reason in this sense has developed since Hooker.

5. See standard commentaries on Mark 10.1–12 and parallels; or the detailed study of biblical evidence in two Church of England reports, *Marriage, Divorce and the Church*, 1971, and *Marriage and the Church's Task*, 1978.

6. I Cor. 6.1ff.

7. Cf. Anthony Thiselton, *The Two Horizons*, 1980.

8. Roman Catholic official documents now pay much more attention to the Bible, but the text is often quoted in a non-contextual way.

9. Karl Barth, *Against the Stream: Shorter Post-War Writings*, 1954, p. 39, para. 22.

10. The arguments were: 1. Slavery was divinely sanctioned among the patriarchs (to which there are many references in Genesis), and it was indeed decreed by God as an institution before it existed (Gen. 9.24–27). 2. Slavery was incorporated into Israel's Torah (again many references), even taking priority over marriage (Ex. 21.2–4). 3. Slavery is recognized in the New Testament; Jesus never condemned it, and the apostolic writings affirm it (whilst criticizing abuses of it); there is no exhortation to masters to free their slaves, not even when Paul sends back Onesimus to Philemon, whilst I Tim. 6.1–4 says that its doctrine on slavery is based on the words of Jesus himself. See J.H. Hopkins, *A Scriptural and Historical View of Slavery from the Days of the Patriarch Abraham to the Nineteenth Century*, 1864. On the other hand, slaves in the USA identified their bondage with that of Israel in Egypt, and their sufferings with those of Jesus (as I Peter 2. 18ff.). See also J.F. Maxwell, *Slavery and the Catholic Church*, 1975. In the same way texts are used today to condemn homosexuality. It is possible to show that their meaning is not always as drastic as it appears, and that some occur in a context of other prohibitions which no one follows precisely today (Lev. 18.23ff.); but it is clear that the biblical writers have no conception of a person who is by 'nature' homosexual, an awareness which came first in this century. Biblical texts by themselves cannot settle the question of homosexuality (or, for that matter, the relation of humans to the rest of nature, another issue much discussed today).

11. *Methodology used to derive Biblical Principles for Issues Relating to the Social Order*, 1988. It is to be noted that evangelicals rarely refer to the so-called 'communism' of the Jerusalem church in its early days, as mentioned at the end of Acts 2 and 4. It appears to have involved a voluntary pooling of wealth by those who had some, on which the whole church lived in expectation of an imminent *parousia* or return of Christ. When this did not happen they had impoverished themselves, and St Paul made a major effort to raise a collection from his Gentile churches for the Jerusalem Christians (II Cor. 8 and 9). It was delivering it that led to his arrest. How does this bear upon us today? Some Christians still expect an imminent *parousia*. I wonder whether they forego insurance and pension contributions? The vast majority have no such expectation. A fundamental problem for Christian ethics is how to maintain a *parousia* radicalism when a *parousia* is not expected. It certainly suggests a sitting loose to income and possessions as a personal attitude, but an economic order must relate to a foreseeable future. (My information on the 'Keep Sunday Special' literature came from a critique in a paper by the Revd Dr W. Houston of Westminster College, Cambridge.)

12. *Economics Today: A Christian Critique*, 1989. Texts quoted are: (i) Gen. 1.18–20; 2.15; 8.22; Matt. 6.25–32; (ii) Luke 19.11–17; (iii) Lev. 25; 1 Kings 21–23; (iv) Gen. 1.28; 2.3; Ps. 104.23; Prov. 6.6; II. Thess. 3.6–13; (v) Gen.

3.12–19; Deut. 24.15; (vi) none quoted; (vii) Gen. 2.16; 3.21; I Tim. 6.8; (viii) Mark 7.23; Luke 12.13–21; 16.19–31.

13. After the Second World War there were several books on work with titles like *The* (sic) *Biblical Doctrine of Work*; now there are similar ones on nature.

14. Justice as fairness becomes a criterion as soon as more than two people are involved, even in a family where all the children are equally loved; how much more is it involved in public, social and political issues. In the New Testament it is latent rather than explicit. Love without justice is sentimental; it needs to be structured, even though the structures never fully express it. Justice without love is legalism. Similarly the language of human rights is not in the Gospels, and some think is opposed to them. But rights are what we must claim for others because of their dignity as persons, and for ourselves for the sake of consistency in policies. Legal and material rights are the basic framework of a life that is proper for those created in God's image.

15. This is sometimes called an 'eschatological reserve'; eschaton refers to the last events in two senses, last or ultimate in significance and last chronologically. Christians believe that events of lasting significance occurred in the ministry of Jesus but that they will be perfected only when time ends. So Christians cannot give unqualified approval to anything less than that; hence the element of reserve in their attitudes.

16. The 'essential' Trinity, stressing God's inmost essence and the 'economic' Trinity, stressing his outreach to us in creation. (This is a quite different sense of the word economic from that with which this book is concerned.)

17. Jürgen Moltmann opts for a brash social doctrine of the Trinity in *The Trinity and the Kingdom of God: The Doctrine of God*, 1981. He even says that each subject of the Trinity possesses his own unique personality (*God in Creation*, 1985, p. 97).

18. Leonardo Boff, *The Trinity and Society*, 1989.

19. Meeks, *God the Economist*, Fortress Press 1989, pp. 132ff.

20. The Old Testament prophets, such as the three Isaiahs and Jeremiah, did not find that monotheism hampered them in denouncing structures of domination, rather the contrary.

21. To cite one only of very many books on natural law I choose A.P. d'Entrèves, *Natural Law* (revised edition), 1970.

22. Thus Moltmann says drastically (*God in Creation*, 1985, p. 12) that the only alternative to universal anihilation is the non-violent, peaceful, ecological world-wide community in solidarity; incongruously his one practical suggestion is that we should leave our cars at home on Sunday so that nature too can celebrate its sabbath (p. 296).

23. It is noteworthy that all the main churches were hostile to contraception until half-way through this century. It was lay Christians who practised it and convinced the theologians and leaders of most churches that it is a responsible way of living married life as Christians.

24. For this middle level see 'Middle Axioms in Christian Social Ethics', in my *Church and Society in the Late Twentieth Century*, 1983, pp. 141–56.

25. This runs counter to the argument that there is no fundamental foundation of rationality or human value to which anyone can appeal

(cf. Alasdair MacIntyre, *After Virtue*, 1981). I am told that in Mandarin Chinese the character which expresses the way people live together in society signifies 'between-ness', and for those who lack this fundamental sense there is another character signifying 'fools'. It is important for Christians to realize that there are adumbrations in 'secular' society of *koinonia*, that word which the New Testament uses of the church, meaning 'persons-in-relationship'; many words in common use bear witness to this, such as community, common, commune, communism, communion, communication (cf. *Changing Britain: Social Diversity and Moral Unity*, a report to the General Synod of the Church of England, Church House Publishing 1987).

26. It is known in classical moral theology as tutiorism, and not approved.

8. North–South: The Responsibilities of Affluence

1. Article 301 of the USA Trade Act of 1974 allows such policies whenever the US government thinks competition is not 'fair'. Japan and Korea, and to a lesser extent the EC are its main targets.

2. *Human Development Report*, a study by the UN Development Programme, 1990. One of its criteria was the number of teachers compared with the number in the armed forces; on this score Costa Rica came first because it has no army.

3. Cf. Peter Bauer, *Equality, the Third World and Economic Delusion*, 1981.

4. Peter Bauer, *Dissent on Development*, 1977.

5. Robert Carson and Associates, *Does Aid Work?* It was independent in its work and findings.

6. It has been calculated that it may take a century to bring many African countries to a desirable economic level; but of course forecasts on that time-scale are very speculative. An example of lack of donor co-ordination is that there are eighteen different makes of pumps in Kenya's water supply system.

7. *Our Common Future*, Report of the World Commission on Environment and Development, 1987. It argues for 'sustainable development'. This involves controlled economic growth, to reduce environmental pressures. The report estimates that over the next fifty years an increase of economic growth between five and ten fold will be needed to deal with mass poverty, and this means a 3% p.a. growth in per capita income in developing countries. It calls for measures to preserve or restore the soil and stocks of water, forest and fish, etc., for the development of resource-conserving technologies through recycling, for a more efficient use of energy, and for a reduction in the rate of growth of population. New international procedures of decision-making need to be devised (a major undertaking). An international tax on the use of the 'global commons' (i.e. ocean fisheries and sea-bed mining) is proposed, together with taxes on international trade. Cf. Frances Cairncross, *Costing the Earth*, 1991, for an economist's approach.

8. Some writers point to the harmony between humans and nature in the ancient religions of the earth among e.g. the Indians of North America, the Aborigines of Australia, and tribal religions in Africa (cf. W. Davies and G. Sessions, *Deep Ecology: Living as if Nature Mattered*, Salt Lake City 1985).

Others praise the religions of the East as against exploitative 'Christian' lands of the 'West'. However, there is much exploitation in Hindu India, whilst the influence of Christianity in the 'West' has been exaggerated, and its teaching has more sides to it than its attackers allow. In fact its range does more justice to the complexities of the situation of humans in nature than the monolithic attitudes of those who attack it. Some Christians accept these criticisms too readily and call for a total change in the attitude to nature in their own tradition, cf. William E. Gibson, 'An Order in Crisis and the Declaration of New Things', in *Reformed Faith and Economics*, ed. R.L. Stevens, University Press of America, Lanham, Md 1989.

9. Cf. Paul Elkins (ed.), *The Living Economy: a New Economics in the Making*, 1986; E.E. Trainer, *Revolution in Affluent Societies*, 1985; Herman E. Daly, *Economics, Ecology and Ethics*, W.H. Freeman, San Francisco 1979; and Charles Birch, *On Purpose*, Sydney 1990. These and other writings mostly reflect an attitude to nature which regards it as a harmonious whole, whereas eco-systems are competitive as well as co-operative and in ceaseless change. Nature commits 'crimes' for which humans would be severely punished.

10. Some form of income guarantee might be tried for Third World agricultural workers, though a quota ceiling would also be needed. International commodity agreements to guarantee incomes by stabilizing the price of basic commodities like coffee, sugar, cocoa and tin have all failed (partly because they cannot prevent import substitutes being sought by First World countries).

11. For the point that it is a Christian task not only to teach sacrifice and forgiveness but also to seek to strengthen the power base of the poor, see Michael Taylor, *Good for the Poor: Christian Ethics and World Development*, 1990.

12. The fact that states do act in this way and have very limited powers of self-transcendence, and that it is only on this basis that structures of international relations and international law can be built, needs to be brought more explicitly into a Christian doctrine of the state as a divine institution for human well-being. It was a constant preoccupation of Reinhold Niebuhr in his books from the early *Moral Man and Immoral Society*, 1932, onwards.

13. *North–South, A Programme for Survival*, 1980, and *Common Crisis North–South: Co-operation for World Recovery*, 1982.

14. A survey of *British Social Attitudes*, Social and Community Planning Research, an independent non-profit institute, 1990, shows a considerable majority in favour of a collective rather than an individualist approach to taxation and welfare, not just targetting to the poorest; half want a redistributive policy from the richer to the poorer. This attitude needs to be extended beyond national frontiers.

Epilogue

1. There is an inevitable ambiguity about the claim of Christian faith as a whole; if it were not so, logic would lead everyone to believe it. Life's experience can be interpreted in more than one way, and a choice has to be made. It was clearly possible totally to misinterpret Jesus' life and ministry. Jesus himself was a man of faith, and he is a prototype of such to all who follow him.

2. Such thinkers often point to the vested interests of the professions and

the 'producer orientated' nature of their professional organizations. This is a valid criticism if they speak as if their concern is chiefly with professional standards and affect to look down on trade unions as selfish and irresponsible. Their dual role is legitimate, but it needs to be avowed.

3. Cf. Chapter 8, 'The New Right: A Theological Critique', in my *The Future of Christian Ethics*, 1987.

4. In my view the best discussion is still Karl Mannheim's *Ideology and Utopia*, ET 1936.

5. The Roman Catholic Bishops of Latin America held their fourth conference (CELAM) in 1992 at Santo Domingo, where Christopher Columbus landed in 1492. In what terms was this celebrated? The 'West' is becoming more sensitive to what it has done to ethnic minorities, e.g. Indians in Canada and the USA, Aborigines in Australia and Maoris in New Zealand.

6. The question of trans-national corporations is an example. I hold no particular brief for them and, indeed, think that their public accountability is a major question of concern. Shareholders can have little effective control; only governments are in a position to exercise checks on their powers, and in certain circumstances they can be more powerful than governments. Some form of international supervision is needed. The evidence on what they do is mixed. There are good and bad points, and there is little agreement among those, Christians included, who investigate them on the verdict to be passed. Those in the Third World are apt to find them a scapegoat for all their woes. Yet four-fifths of the Third World is beyond the scope of their activities (their impact is mainly in cities); and most of their trade is within the First World.

7. Cf. Chapter 7.

8. A brief treatment on the limitations of apocalyptic can be found in Chapter 9, 'Reflections on Theologies of Social Change', in *Theology and Change*, 1975, a symposium which I edited.

9. The ideologies of imperfection and political scepticism often associated with Conservatism and of utopia often associated with Socialism are more fully treated in Chapter 12, 'The Politics of Imperfection and the Politics of Hope', in my *The Future of Christian Ethics*, 1987.

Appendix 1: Usury and a Christian Ethic of Finance

1. Jacob Viner, *Religious Thought and Economic Society*, ed. J. Melitz and D. Walsh, Duke University Press, Durham NC 1978, see esp. 111f.

2. The most thorough treatment of the subject in John T. Noonan Jr, *The Scholastic Analysis of Usury*, 1958. It was preceded by Bernard W. Dempsey, *Interest and Usury*, 1948, and followed by the second and enlarged edition of Benjamin Nelson, *The Idea of Usury: from Tribal Brotherhood to Universal Otherhood* (1946), University of Chicago Press. 1969.

3. Islam has had the same problem. In the Qur'an there is a prohibition of *ribā*, and there has been a debate throughout the history of Islam as to whether or not it covers all interest. In the Prophet's day, as in biblical times and early mediaeval Europe, loans were rarely for venture capital but for consumption. Charity was preferred for the latter, notably through the *zakat* or $2\frac{1}{2}\%$ assessment on most assets held for at least a year. A distinction tends to be

made between an entrepreneur who earns his reward by risk-taking decisions and a capitalist who merely provides money and is paid for waiting. The mutual Islamic banking system involves shared profits rather than a fixed rate of interest, that is to say rewarding the bank for its entrepreneurial function; but in fact it is still being paid for waiting.

4. D.H. Meadows, J. Randers and W.W. Behrens, *The Limits to Growth*, 1972.

5. A recent example is R.J. Hinkelammert, *The Ideological Weapons of Death: A Theological Critique of Capitalism*, ET Maryknoll, New York 1986. The first of the three parts of the book is taken up with a detailed exposition of Marx's analysis of fetishism from *Das Kapital*, assumed to be an accurate tool for analysing capitalism. The case that Marx's economic theories are the weakest part of his work is not mentioned.

6. R.H. Tawney, *Religion and the Rise of Capitalism* (1926), 1929, p. 88.

7. Thomas Wilson, *A Discourse upon Usury*, ed. R.H. Tawney, 1925, pp. 165ff.

8. Tawney, *Religion and Rise of Capitalism* (n. 6), p. 185.

9. Noonan, *Scholastic Analysis of Usury* (n. 2), p. 408.

10. Alan Storkey, *Transforming Economics: A Christian Way to Employment*, 1986.

11. Ibid., p. 171.

12. Ibid., p. 180.

13. Ibid., pp. 184–91.

14. *Economic Justice for All: Catholic Social Teaching on the USA Economy*, Washington 1986.

15. Ronald H. Preston, *Religion and the Persistence of Capitalism*, 1979, chapters 1–4; Michael H. Taylor (ed.), *Christians and the Future of Social Democracy*, 1982, chapter 2; Ronald H. Preston, *Church and Society in the Late Twentieth Century: The Economic and Political Tasks*, 1983, chapters 1–3.

16. *Religion and Persistence of Capitalism* (n. 15), pp. 48f.

17. J. Philip Wogaman, *A Christian Method of Moral Judgment*, 1976, Chapters 2, 3, 4.

18. *Summa Theologiae* 2–2 qu. 66 art 8.

19. Dempsey, *Interest and Usury* (n. 2), pp. 212, 222, 225.

Index